JUST LIKE US

JUST LIKE US
21 Character Studies
from the Bible

by

J. Oswald Sanders

MOODY PRESS

CHICAGO

Moody Press, a ministry of the Moody Bible Institute, is designed for
education, evangelization, and edification. If we may assist you in knowing more about Christ and the Christian life, please write us without
obligation: Moody Press, c/o MLM, Chicago, Illinois 60610.

Library of Congress Cataloging-in-Publication Data

Sanders, J. Oswald (John Oswald), 1902-
    Just like us.

    Previously published as: People just like us.
    Bibliography: p.
    Includes indexes.
    1. Bible — Biography.   I. Title.
BS571.S233   1985   220.9′2 [B]   85-15439
ISBN 0-8024-6516-1 (pbk.)

3 4 5 6 7 Printing BC Year 88

Printed in the United States of America

Contents

Introduction

It is not without significance that so large a proportion of the Bible is devoted to biography. The Scriptures are inspired by God; He has therefore given biographies in the form in which we find them so that we can learn valuable spiritual lessons from the failures and successes of these real men and women. Many Christians learn much more from the study of people than from the study of doctrine.

There is much to be learned, too, from the minor characters of Scripture—as well as from the spiritual giants of the past. The former come much closer to our own level. Bible biography is greatly condensed, but it can give a realistic picture of a person and disclose his essential personality in a sentence. Under the guidance of the Holy Spirit, Scripture writers mastered the Greek ideal of "an ocean of meaning in a drop of speech."

Human biographers are inclined to include the best and to omit or treat lightly any deficiencies or delinquencies. Not all of us are as uncompromising as was Oliver Cromwell when he laid down the terms on which he would grant a sitting to Lely, the painter: "Mr. Lely, I desire you would use all your skill to paint my picture truly like me, and not flatter me at all; but remark all these roughnesses, pimples, warts, and everything as you see me, otherwise I will never pay a farthing for it."

Bible biographers include the roughnesses, pimples, and warts. They portray their characters precisely as they were. They tell that Abraham was the friend of God, but also that he twice imperiled his wife's virtue through lying. They record Noah's walking with God, but also his getting drunk. How grateful we should be for this earthly realism that refuses to put the saints on an ivory pedestal, but rather depicts them as men "subject to like passions as we are" (James 5:17, KJV*).

In his *Stones of Venice*, Ruskin wrote, "No man is without a divinely-appointed task, and a divinely-bestowed strength adequate for its fulfillment." In the character studies of this book, these two things are matched; but some of the characters failed because they did not appropriate the divinely bestowed strength.

The persons chosen for study can hardly be called the major characters of the Bible, as the major characters have been treated in the author's book *Bible Men of Faith*. But here are men and women of stature nevertheless, and their lives well repay study.

To get the best out of these studies, you should read them Bible in hand. Copious references are given for the help of Sunday school teachers and group leaders.

In the foreword to his book *The Greatest Men of the Bible*, Clarence Edward Macartney, one of America's great preachers of the past generation, had this to say: "Early in my first pastorate, at the First Presbyterian Church, Paterson, New Jersey, I made the important homiletic discovery that the people like to hear sermons on Bible characters, and that the preacher can preach on Bible characters more naturally, fluently, and practically than on any other subject."[1] Perhaps this book will encourage some preachers to embark on a series on characters of the Bible.

---

*King James Version.

1. Clarence Edward Macartney, *The Greatest Men of the Bible* (New York: Abingdon-Cokesbury, 1941), p. 5.

OLD TESTAMENT

1

Noah

A Man or a Myth?

"Noah walked with God. . . . Noah . . . planted a vine-yard. And he drank of the wine and became drunk" (Genesis 6:9; 9:20-21).

The significance of the rainbow which God spanned over Noah's altar of prayer as a perpetual promise (Genesis 9:13) is lost unless we put ourselves back to the age of the patriarchs. As Henry Vaughan puts it:

> How bright wert thou, when Shem's admiring eye
> Thy burnisht, flaming Arch did first descry!
> When Terah, Nahor, Haran, Abram, Lot,
> The youthful world's grey fathers in one knot,
> Did with intentive looks watch every hour
> For thy new light, and trembled at each shower![1]
>
> (Samuel Marinus Zwemer)

Noah and his ark and Jonah and the whale have been the butts of rationalistic ridicule over the years. The histories of both men and the surrounding events have been challenged and dismissed with a patronizing smile as in-

1. Samuel Marinus Zwemer, *Sons of Adam* (Grand Rapids: Baker, 1951), p. 91.

teresting legends that might convey some moral lessons.

Despite the cynicism of theologians and scientists as to the authenticity of the accounts of Noah and the deluge, investigators of ancient legends have made discoveries that indicate the biblical narrative might not be so lacking in factual basis as is often alleged. A great number of stories strikingly similar to the Genesis account have been unearthed. Traditional memories of a great flood occur among peoples of advanced civilization as well as in very primitive groups, and this in widely scattered lands.

Professor J. Riem of the Institute for Astronomical Calculation, Berlin, assembled legends from more than three hundred sources. In those sources, the main features of the biblical narrative frequently occur. He reports that in fifty-three cases the cause of the deluge is said to be man's wickedness; in twenty-two, the anger of God. The ark appears seventy-two times as a boat or ship. Twenty-three times men are warned to prepare for coming disaster. Forty-two times a mountain on which the ark landed is mentioned. In ten cases the sending out of the birds from the ark is spoken of; in twenty-one cases the rainbow appears. In thirty-one cases the deluge is associated with the creation story.[2]

As these legends emanate from India, China, Europe, Africa, Australia, and the Americas, this universal tradition with its similarity to the biblical narrative requires some explanation. Surely so widespread and persistent a tradition cannot be dismissed in cavalier fashion as an invention or a myth. If it be suggested that these are only survivals of missionary propaganda, the answer is that the stories are too widespread; and in any case they antedate the missionary enterprise.

This is not the place for a discussion of the extent of the flood, but it may be stated in passing that the case has been keenly argued both for a universal inundation and for a local flood, the latter affecting only that part of the earth that was then inhabited. Genesis 7:19 favors a uni-

2. J. Riem, *The Deluge in Legend and Science* (Hamburg: Agentur des Rauhen Haus, 1926).

versal deluge: "And the water prevailed more and more upon the earth, so that all the high mountains everywhere under the heavens were covered."

The Historicity of Noah

Noah's name appears with other historical characters in the genealogy of Genesis 5:28-32. He thus has the same claim to a place in history as Adam or Enoch. He was the son of Lamech, who came of the line of Seth. The whole record treats him as a historical personage, as does the prophet Ezekiel (Ezekiel 14:14).

As if this were not sufficient, the Lord Himself adds His testimony: "The coming of the Son of Man will be just like the days of Noah. For as in those days which were before the flood they were eating and drinking, they were marrying and giving in marriage, until the day that Noah entered the ark" (Matthew 24:37-38). Noah. The flood. The ark. Thus our omniscient Lord stamped the biblical narrative with His endorsement of its historicity. To deny that endorsement is to charge Him with either ignorance or mendacity.

If we are to arrive at a correct appraisal of this great character of antiquity, we must understand the times in which he lived. The earth was shrouded in deep moral and spiritual darkness. Note the divine diagnosis: "The wickedness of man was great on the earth, and . . . every intent of the thoughts of his heart was only evil continually. . . . The earth was corrupt in the sight of God, and the earth was filled with violence" (Genesis 6:5, 11).

With the exception of Noah and his family, human depravity was total. Society had become so corrupt that God repented of His creation (Genesis 6:6, KJV). It is with relief that we turn to the contrasting character of Noah: "Noah found favor in the eyes of the LORD. . . . Noah was a righteous man, blameless in his time; Noah walked with God" (Genesis 6:8-9).

God confided to Noah that the race had become so depraved that the only hope was to make an "end of all flesh" (Genesis 6:13) and begin again. But with the announcement of judgment there was also opportunity for repentance and deliverance: "Behold, I am about to destroy them [all flesh] with the earth. Make for yourself an ark of gopher wood" (Genesis 6:13-14).

The use in the King James Version of the word "repented" in connection with God has given rise to misconception. God is not capricious and changeable, and most modern versions give the more accurate meaning "was sorry." God is here accommodating Himself to the limitations of human language. The simple meaning of the passage is that because of man's irreversible corruption, God was about to alter His procedure towards mankind and execute judgment on it.

The conditions that led up to this judgment are somewhat mysterious. "The sons of God saw that the daughters of men were beautiful; and they took wives for themselves, whomever they chose" (Genesis 6:2). The intermarriage of these two strains, whatever they were, apparently issued in the corruption and violence that called down divine judgment.

Some have taken "the sons of God" to refer to spirit beings from the other world who married beautiful women of the human race. This interpretation raises insuperable difficulties. Nowhere in Scripture are evil angels called sons of God, and good angels would not commit this sin. Some supporters of this view appeal to Jude 6-7 for support. But those verses could be interpreted as meaning that "the sin of the fallen angels was spiritually what that of Sodom was carnally."[3] Human kings were sometimes called "sons of God," and it would seem "more natural and Scriptural to regard the 'sons of God' as the pious Sethites."[4]

Noah and his sons commenced to build the ark in keeping with the divinely given specifications. The dimensions, 450 feet by 75 feet by 45 feet, would make it a vessel of about eighteen thousand tons. Marine engineers have

---

3. W. G. Moorehead, *Outline Studies in the Old Testament* (1893; reprint ed., Grand Rapids: Zondervan, n.d.), p. 21.
4. Ibid.

stated that those proportions would make the vessel graceful, safe, and not significantly different from a modern ship. It had three decks, the lower one doubtless accomodating the great stores of fodder required, which would serve as ballast.

If, as has been contended, there was no such vessel, the fact that the correct proportions for a vessel of that size were known requires some explanation. In his *Jewish Antiquities*, Josephus, a Roman historian, stated that in his day (A.D. 90) the remains of the bitumen sealed ark could be seen on the slopes of Mount Ararat. Even in recent years similar reports have been made, and expeditions mounted to verify them, but thus far without success.

A Lengthy Sermon

For one hundred and twenty years, Noah, his sons, and their helpers toiled to build the ark; and for one hundred and twenty years, "Noah, a preacher of righteousness" (2 Peter 2:5), bore testimony to the impending judgment. This lengthy period must be understood both in the light of the longevity of men in those days and in the light of the magnitude of the task. Noah was six hundred years old when the deluge began.

The construction of the ark is the longest, most drawn-out test of faith recorded in the Bible. Throughout the whole period, Noah's hard-pressed faith was given no visible confirmation. His conviction that a flood was coming was shared by no one but his own family. Public opinion was solidly against him. There was no precedent to which he could appeal for reassurance. Never before had there been a flood. Both nature and experience were against its probability. Noah was regarded as an eccentric and his sons as fools. But in blind, unquestioning faith the man who walked with God accepted God's revelation and acted on it. "Thus Noah did; according to all that God had commanded him, so he did" (Genesis 6:22). His was a sublime faith and obedience.

With the vivid picture drawn by divine inspiration before us, there is little need to enlarge on the awfulness of the tragedy of the deluge—the terror of man and beast as the waters relentlessly rose, the sudden change in the people from ridicule to belief, the unavailing endeavors to enter the ark when it was too late. Outside the ark, there was nothing but death and destruction. Within the ark, the people of faith were borne up above the waters of judgment.

When at length the water subsided and Noah with his family emerged from the ark, his genuine piety was manifested in his first action. "Then Noah built an altar to the LORD . . . and offered burnt offerings" (Genesis 8:20) as an expression of worship and gratitude for deliverance. This, the first altar of Scripture, was a tacit indication of Noah's consciousness of his need of atonement for his sin.

The Rainbow Covenant

God graciously responded by entering into a perpetual convenant with Noah and his descendants as they entered this new era of world history: "I establish My covenant with you; and all flesh shall never again be cut off by the water of the flood. . . . I set my bow in the cloud, . . . then I will look upon it, to remember the everlasting covenant between God and every living creature of all flesh that is on the earth" (Genesis 9:11, 13, 16). This divine undertaking would banish fear that there might be a repetition of the terrible judgment.

To those who had faith in God's promise, the rainbow brought reassurance concerning the future. Never again would the course of nature be so drastically interrupted in that way. It was appropriate that God should choose the sign of the rainbow. Its beauty, its universality, and its perpetuity make it a singularly felicitous symbol of God's grace and mercy. The record does not necessarily imply that the rainbow had never appeared before; but it was now invested with new significance, a visible pledge of a divine promise. The rainbow brings its message to us today.

"There is never rain without a rainbow being visible if

we could only get to the right spot to see it," wrote Eugene Stock. "But God is always above the clouds and He always sees it."[5]

With this background we can obtain a clearer view of the stature of this man of God. He was one of the two men of whom it is written, he "walked with God" (Genesis 5:24; 6:9). His intimacy with God assures us that it is possible to walk in constant fellowship with God in an adverse spiritual climate. Noah's walk necessarily took him in the same direction as God, and it thus involved a break with his contemporaries who were traveling in the opposite direction. Walking with God is a privilege open to all, but He thrusts His company on no one.

Faith in Sordid Times

Noah is marked out among the great characters of history by divine eulogy: "You alone I have seen to be righteous before Me in this time" (Genesis 7:1). Because of his faith, he, like Abraham, was accounted righteous. The very sordidness of the times in which he lived made his lamp of witness shine the more brightly. He was not only *accounted* righteous, he *was* righteous. "Noah was . . . blameless in his time" (Genesis 6:9); that is, he was morally upright, a man of stainless integrity. Because of this, "Noah found favor in the eyes of the LORD" (Genesis 6:8).

The motivation behind his astounding achievement appears in Hebrews 11:7. "Noah, being warned by God about things not yet seen, in reverence prepared an ark for the salvation of his household, by which he condemned the world, and became an heir of the righteousness which is according to faith." He was not frightened of God, but he reverenced Him, and that moved him to incredible heights of faith and achievement.

Because he stood in awe of God, he became "a preacher [herald] of righteousness" (2 Peter 2:5) who inveighed against the corruption and violence of his age. Our genera-

---

5. Quoted in W. H. Griffith Thomas, *Genesis: A Devotional Commentary* (n.d., reprint ed., Grand Rapids: Eerdmans, 1953), p. 93.

tion could well do with another Noah to be the conscience of our society as Noah was to his. What persevering faith he exercised—a hundred years of preaching and not a single convert! And what of the workmen who spent years toiling on the great ship, observing Noah's godly life and hearing his faithful witness? Because they did not believe, they perished outside the refuge they themselves had helped to build.

As a powerful intercessor, Noah was bracketed with Daniel and Job, two of the most blameless characters of ancient history. Ezekiel, a contemporary of Daniel, selected those three men, cited them as examples of righteous, prayerful men, and used them to illustrate the solemn fact that the evil of men can reach a point beyond which even the prayers of such godly intercessors cannot avert judgment (Ezekiel 14:14, 20).

Noah's unwavering faith won for him a place of honor in God's hall of fame. It was "by faith Noah . . . prepared an ark . . . and became an heir of the righteousness which is according to faith" (Hebrews 11:7). His faith was not academic. It moved him to activity that imposed tremendous demands on his confidence in God. The test was the more stringent because he had to tread the path of faith alone. His very nonconformity to the prevailing evil condemned his fellow citizens and "put the whole world in the wrong" (Hebrews 11:7, NEB*).

A Clouded Sunset

There is deep pathos in the fact that after so magnificent an achievement Noah's sun should set in partial eclipse. But Bible history is realistic, and Noah was neither the first nor the last saint to experience failure in the last lap of the race. The best of men are fallible and liable to fall before the subtle attacks of the enemy.

Two sentences express the trauma of this page of Noah's history: "Noah built an altar to the LORD . . . Noah . . . planted a vineyard" (Genesis 8:20; 9:20). The Lord met

* *New English Bible.*

him at the altar. The devil seduced him in the vineyard. The man who walked with God proved to be a man subject to like passions as we are, and he became the first intoxicated man mentioned in Scripture.

The charitable view of this incident is that although it is a regrettable stain on a wonderful record, Noah's drunkenness was an accident and not a blameworthy act. He was ignorant of the potency of the wine and foolishly drank too much. Moral delinquency is not necessarily involved or implied.

This is a possible explanation, but there are other factors that could involve culpability. The word "drank" (Genesis 9:21) means "to drink deeply," and the idea of indulgence is not excluded. It can further be argued that a man walking in close fellowship with God, as was Noah's habit, is seldom ensnared in a situation about which he had no premonition of evil.

Satan lays his snares skillfully. How he must have gloated when he saw the world's greatest saint, a man on whom God's hopes were fixed, lying on the ground naked and drunk. After long years of discipline, in a moment of laxity, Noah was found to have a chink in his armor; and the adversary launched his fiery dart. Alas, the shield of faith was not in Noah's hand, and he was smitten.

No One Sins in Isolation

No one sins in isolation. Noah's sin affected the whole family. The effects of Noah's lack of self-control were tragic. In a drunken stupor, he lay uncovered in his tent; his son Ham, devoid of filial respect and decency, made lewd fun of his father's shame. In contrast, Shem and Japheth showed respect and modesty. Noah's stricken reaction to Ham's disrespect called forth a prophetic utterance, the fulfillment of which can be seen today (see Genesis 9:25-27).

Throughout the ages, the black Hamitic races have tended to be oppressed. The Jewish and Arab Semitic races have been the custodians of religion and religious teaching. The Aryan and Anglo-Saxon Japhetic races

have been the great explorers, colonizers, and popula-
tors—and missionaries.

From this unhappy incident—and the last three hundred and fifty years of Noah's life are passed over in silence—some lessons of permanent application emerge:
The hour of victory and achievement can be the hour of
danger. We never progress beyond the reach of temptation.
It is never safe to doff our armor. Temptation will meet us
in the course of our legitimate occupations, and we never
know when or where the next temptation may strike. Believers can be the occasion of sin to others.

2

Sarah

The Woman Who Laughed

"Sarah laughed to herself. . . . And the LORD said, . . . 'Why did Sarah laugh? . . .' Sarah denied it however, saying, 'I did not laugh' " (Genesis 18:12-13, 15).

"And Sarah said, 'God has made laughter for me; everyone who hears will laugh with me' " (Genesis 21:6).

We can never be too careful against falling into the old sin. One might well imagine that after the bitter experience in Egypt, Sarah would never again consent to act a lie. It was a sharp lesson for both the woman and her husband, and yet we find them falling exactly where they had fallen before. . . . When we think of the repeated lapse of good people like Abraham and Sarah, we are reminded that we can place no trust in ourselves.[1]

(Donald Davidson)

It was in no backward and primitive Eastern village that Abraham and his wife Sarai lived. The city of Ur was an important commercial center, strategically placed at the

1. Donald Davidson, *Mothers in the Bible* (London: Marshall, Morgan & Scott, 1934), p. 18.

crossroads of the East. Theirs was an advanced civilization, with education and commerce highly developed, for Ur was regarded as the cultural center of that day.

At one of the schools that was unearthed there, it was discovered that not only had the inhabitants employed an elaborate form of writing, but also they had developed a system of advanced mathematics. Houses were large and well equipped, even to running water in lavatories. It was the site of the vast ziggurat temple where the moon-god Nama was worshiped.

It must have been a tremendous upheaval to Sarah, at the age of sixty-five, to leave all this comfort and luxury and join her husband in a seemingly aimless, nomadic life. She did not even know where they were going. From the record, it would appear that she did not fully share Abraham's spiritual insights and outlook. Without doubt this step of faith was much more costly to her than to her husband, and it is to her credit that she was prepared to go.

Sarah was an unusually attractive woman. Her husband certainly thought so. "I know that you are a beautiful woman," he said. When Abraham and Sarah fled to Egypt, the officials "saw that the woman was very beautiful." She was so striking that they "saw her and praised her to Pharaoh" (Genesis 12:11, 14, 15). In the Dead Sea Scrolls, reference is made to the beauty of her eyes and the radiance of her face. She was obviously a woman at whom men would look twice. As she lived to the age of one hundred and twenty-seven, when she left Ur she would have been comparatively much younger than a woman of the same age today.

A Happy Marriage Union

The married life of Abraham and Sarah was rendered happy by a mutual love and respect. Abraham was a strict monogamist, and it was not until Sarah's disastrous mistake in giving Hagar to Abraham as a secondary wife that the peace of their home was disturbed. Peter writes of their relationship in a commendatory way: "Thus Sarah obeyed Abraham, calling him lord" (1 Peter 3:6). Her attitude reflected the best cultural pattern of her day.

The names of both Abram and Sarai were changed at the same time. Abram, meaning "exalted father," became Abraham, "father of a multitude of nations" (Genesis 17:5). Sarai (the meaning of her name is doubtful) became Sarah, "my princess," in the sense of mother of the nation (Genesis 17:15-16). This would indicate her high social standing.

According to Genesis 20:12, Sarah was Abraham's half sister, being the daughter of his father but not of his mother. Their relationship lent some color of right to his claim that she was his sister, although it was not all the truth. He had good reason to be proud of his beautiful wife, but her beauty provided the occasion of two lamentable lapses in morality.

The Peril of a Half-Truth

Famine drove Abraham and Sarah down to Egypt, but that was not the land to which God was directing their steps (Genesis 12:1). Knowing the way of Eastern kings, Abraham was fearful for Sarah, and incidentally for himself, so he resorted to deceit to save his own skin. "Please say that you are my sister," he counseled Sarah, "so that it may go well with me because of you, and that I may live on account of you" (Genesis 12:12-13). Thus the friend of God descended from the lofty plane of faith to the low road of expediency. He was willing to sacrifice his wife's virtue in the interest of his own safety. True, it was only a half-lie that he told. Sarah was his half sister, but she was also his wife.

Lying does not admit of degrees; a half-truth is a whole lie. Not only was his action unworthy in itself, but it was also the occasion of possible sin to others (Genesis 12:18), and it brought dishonor on God's name. Only divine intervention prevented tragedy, and Abraham received a well-deserved rebuke from a pagan king.

If we had not experienced the intricacy and subtlety of our own hearts, we might well think that such a salutary experience would have taught Abraham and Sarah a lifelong lesson. But have we had no experience of repeating the same failure after having known God's forgiving grace? It is a fact of experience that former sins do not always lie down and die. They have a remarkable facility for revival.

The sins of youth tend to reassert themselves, perhaps in a more subtle way, in maturer years. It was so with Abraham. He fell into the old snare, and not only did he again involve Sarah, but he also imperiled the king on his throne (Genesis 20). Once again God intervened to deliver His children, and He commanded Abimelech: "Now therefore restore the man's wife. . . . But if you do not restore her, know that you shall surely die, you and all who are yours" (Genesis 20:7). We can never measure how far the effects of a single sin may extend.

When Abraham was seventy-five years old, and Sarah ten years his junior, they were still childless. But after his noble act of renunciation following his victory over the five kings (Genesis 14:22-24), God met him and promised him a son and heir (Genesis 15:4-5). Sarah was not included in the promise at that stage, which fact might have influenced her suggestion that Abraham should take her maid, Hagar, as a wife. Later she was included in the promise as the mother of the promised son and of the Hebrew nation. How often they would talk and plan the future of their long-promised heir.

A Carnal Expedient

The years crawled by on leaden feet. Still there was no response from God, and all natural hopes had faded. At Sarah's instigation, Abraham took matters into his own hands—always a risky procedure for a child of God. Sarah's suggestion that he take Hagar as a secondary wife would be highly irregular today, but it was not so then.

It was repugnant to the later ideas of the Hebrews, but the practice conformed to the Code of Hammurabi and other laws familiar to Abraham. One provision of the Code of Hammurabi states: "If a man has married a wife and she has not given him children, if that man marries his concubine and brings her into his house, then that concubine shall not rank with his wife." This was probably in Sarah's mind when she suggested a method for the longing of Abraham's heart to be gratified. Incidentally, the word "wife" used of Hagar in Genesis 16:3 was used in countries where polygamy prevailed to describe an inferior, though not degrading, relationship.

God was moving too slowly for Abraham and Sarah, but He will not be manipulated or hurried. In His dealings with men, He jealously keeps the time factor in His own hands. Sarah and her husband were to master the art of waiting for God, but they learned the lesson the hard way. It never pays to adopt carnal means to achieve spiritual ends.

According to the laws of that time, a son born to a secondary wife like Hagar was regarded as the heir of the father. So when Hagar discovered that she was to have a child, she became insolent to her childless mistress. When Sarah reacted by ill-treating her, the situation became intolerable, and Hagar fled. Sarah bitterly repented of her attempts to help God fulfill His promise.

As the result of an angelic message, Hagar returned to her mistress and Ishmael was born. But fourteen more years were to elapse before the birth of the promised heir. It was never God's intention that Ishmael should be heir, "for the son of the bondwoman shall not be an heir with the son of the free woman" (Galatians 4:30).

When God repeated to Abraham His promise of a son by Sarah, "Abraham fell on his face and laughed, and said in his heart, 'Will a child be born to a man one hundred years old? And will Sarah, who is ninety years old, bear a child?' " (Genesis 17:17). If his laugh was not that of absolute unbelief, it sprang out of a very imperfect and trembling faith. God did not rebuke him as He did Sarah, but He firmly denied his request that Ishmael might be his heir. He promised Hagar, however, that Ishmael too would become the head of a great nation (Genesis 17:20). Probably as a gentle rebuke to Abraham's incredulous laughter, God reiterated His promise and added, "You shall call his name Isaac [i.e., 'laughter']" (Genesis 17:19).

In ancient times God sometimes adopted theophany, an appearance of God to man in actual manifestation, as a method of Self-revelation, and this He did with Abraham and Sarah. One day Abraham was sitting at his tent door at Mamre when three strangers approached. With typical Oriental courtesy he welcomed them and offered hospitality. While culinary preparations were in progress, one of the men asked about Sarah by name and made reference to the divine promise of a son by a specified date (Genesis 18:9-10). This made Abraham realize that these were no ordinary visitors. Where did they obtain the knowledge of this secret?

The Laughter of Unbelief

From her place behind the partition in the flimsy tent, Sarah heard the conversation and "laughed to herself, saying, 'After I have become old, shall I have pleasure, my lord being old also?' " (Genesis 18:12). The incongruity and incredibility of the suggestion was too much for her, and her inner unbelief found expression in incredulous laughter.

Then "*the* Lord said to Abraham, 'Why did Sarah laugh? . . . Is anything too difficult for the Lord?' " (Genesis 18:13-14, italics added). As Sarah for the first and only time was addressed by God, she was filled with fear and made a hasty denial: "I did not laugh" (Genesis 18:15). She realized intuitively that she was in the presence of God and had reason to fear. There was some truth in her denial, for there had been no *outward* expression of her unbelief. The fact that her unvoiced laughter was known to this mysterious Stranger, even though she was not visible to Him, filled her with awe.

The divine rebuke of her long-standing unbelief was just what she needed to awaken faith. She had thought that some things were too difficult for the Lord, but it would seem that from this time onward Sarah embraced and held fast to the promise.

Twenty-five years after the promise was first given, it was fulfilled. A sanctified imagination will enable us to enter a little into the magnitude of the test to Sarah's faith, but it ended in laughter. Isaac was born. The impossible became reality.

In her joy Sarah cried, "God has made laughter for me;

everyone who hears will laugh with me" (Genesis 21:6). This time it was the laugh of joy at the vindication of her faith. Feeble at first, her faith grew until it won for her a place among the heroes and heroines of faith. "By faith even Sarah herself received ability to conceive, even beyond the proper time of life, since she considered Him faithful who had promised" (Hebrews 11:11). Her faith blossomed late, even if she never rose to the sublime heights attained by her husband.

This is encouraging for those who are older. Exploits of faith are not reserved only for the young, for Sarah was at least ninety years old at the time she gave birth. On the other hand, had she believed God's promise earlier she would have been spared the tragedy of Hagar and the tragedy of the years of gloom that resulted.

The Supreme Test

The story of Sarah's life would not be complete without some reference to the offering of Isaac on Mount Moriah, when Abraham's faith and surrender reached their zenith. So far as the record goes, Abraham did not take either Sarah or Isaac into his confidence as he set out on the fateful journey. It is difficult to believe, however, that she did not discern from her husband's preoccupation that this was no ordinary journey. Did she as well as Isaac notice that Abraham took no lamb with him?

If she did know the facts, she showed a great consecration to the will of God in offering no objection to the divine demand. Her faith in the promise of God was now so strong that if Abraham believed God could raise her son from dead (Hebrews 11:19), so did she, "since she considered Him faithful who had promised" (Hebrews 11:11). Now she believed that nothing was too difficult for the Lord. Josephus tells of a legend that when Abraham and Isaac returned from Moriah, they found Sarah dying of a broken heart, but of course this has no scriptural support.

The possession of a family burial-ground is of great importance to Eastern peoples, but Abraham's nomadic life had prevented him from acquiring even a burial place. In his notable address, Stephen referred to the fact that God "gave him [Abraham] no inheritance in it [the promised land], not even a foot of ground" (Acts 7:5).

When Sarah died at the age of one hundred and twenty-seven, Abraham bought the cave of Machpelah as a burial place, and tenderly laid his princess to rest. It is of interest that Sarah, the mother of the Hebrew people, is the only woman whose age, death, and burial are mentioned in the Scriptures.

3

Isaac

The Man Who Loved His Food

"Isaac said, . . . 'Hunt game for me; and prepare a savory dish for me such as I love, and bring it to me that I may eat, so that my soul may bless you before I die' " (Genesis 27:2-4).

> In comparison with Abraham's pioneering pilgrimage and friendship with God, Isaac's life was only secondarily religious; it was a secondhand and even second-rated faith compounded of awe, acquiescence and great memories.[1]
>
> (R. E. O. White)

Imagine the strain of living in a world peopled solely with Elijahs and Peters and Marthas! The restfulness of a Mary, the quiet seriousness of a Lazrus, the placidity of an Isaac would be a welcome addition to such a society.

In His wisdom, God has recorded for our instruction the biographies not only of aggressive activists, but also of godly though rather ordinary characters. Isaac falls into this category. He is better known by what he failed to do than by his achievements. Between the towering figures of

1. R. E. O. White, *The Exploration of Faith* (Chicago: Moody, 1969), p. 65.

Abraham the friend of God and Jacob the shrewd schemer comes this rather unimpressive man. He was of a quiet and reflective temperament, lacking in spectacular gifts. His great distinction was that he lacked distinction. The small triumphs he achieved were of a passive nature.

"One of the most important lessons of the Bible," wrote John B. Job, "is the great variety of psychological types that were used by God at different stages in the development of His plan. And this variety is seen in the disciples of Jesus—as striking a mixture as could ever be imagined in twelve men."[2]

Those of us who come from the Occident should note that the scale of virtues of the East contrasts strongly with those of the West. To the Oriental, the passive virtues such as patience and filial piety rank high above the enterprising, activist qualities so admired in the West. And who shall say that they are not right? Judged by this standard, Isaac would stand much higher in the esteem of Oriental society than in our own. Long before the Sermon on the Mount was delivered, Isaac qualified for one of the Beatitudes, for did not Jesus say that it was the meek who inherited the earth, not the pugnacious?

The very fact that Isaac was rather commonplace brings him closer to most of us than are many of the massive characters who made Bible history. He provides us with an example of the manner in which faith operates in a quiet and rather negative nature. There are many such men and women who make an important contribution in the fellowship of the church.

Dwarfed by a Great Father

The birth of Isaac was a momentous event, for it was in fulfillment of a twenty-five-year-old promise. It was a miracle of divine intervention that was heralded by angels. On this birth hung the eternal purpose of God for the blessing of the world, for God had promised Abraham, "In

2. John B. Job, "Isaac," *The Christian and Christianity Today,* Jan. 26, 1968, p. 10.

your seed all the nations of the earth shall be blessed" (Genesis 22:18).

It was Isaac's misfortune to be dwarfed by a great father and a brilliant though devious son, Jacob; and that misfortune left scars on Isaac's personality. He became a follower rather than a leader. Living as he did for forty years under parental domination, he failed to develop the wholesome independence of character so necessary to a mature individual. The very qualities that made his father great stunted the growth of Isaac and produced a rather colorless personality. Not for a moment would we denigrate a godly parentage, but everyone has to meet and do battle with his own enemies and weaknesses, no matter how noble his parents.

After Abraham's strong hand was removed by death, his enemies soon discovered the weakness and passivity of his son and heir. The Philistines exploited these to the full, forcing Isaac to retreat into the wilderness and hill country and stopping all the wells Abraham had dug. The problem was not so much that Isaac was poor-spirited as that when faced with the alternatives of peace or victory, he was so constituted that he always opted for peace.

A revealing sidelight on his character is thrown by Genesis 24:63. "And Isaac went out to meditate in the field toward evening." It was apparently his practice to devote the beautiful evening hour to devout meditation and prayer. He reveled in the solitudes of nature, enjoying fellowship with nature's God.

A Prosperous Agriculturalist

His life was not so negative that he achieved no great success as a farmer, for we read, "Isaac sowed in that land, and reaped in the same year a hundredfold [not one hundred percent, but ten thousand percent!]. And the Lord blessed him, and the man became rich, and continued to grow richer until he became very wealthy; for he had possessions of flocks and herds and a great household" (Genesis 26:12-14). His spectacular prosperity naturally aroused the envy of his hereditary enemies the Philistines.

But it also caused King Abimelech to bear this testimony: "We see plainly that the LORD has been with you" (Genesis 26:28).

It has often been remarked that Isaac was lacking in originality. Abraham dug new wells as he went from place to place—Isaac only reopened the wells that his father had dug and the enemy had stopped. This is true; but, on the other hand, he displayed an undiscourageable perseverance that prevailed in the end. Aggressiveness and pugnacity are not the only methods. Abraham would doubtless have strenuously resisted the enemy activity. Jacob would have outmaneuvered them. But in the end Isaac's less flamboyant tactics secured for him all the water he needed for his extensive farming ventures.

It is an interesting fact that "the naming of wells by Abraham, and the hereditary right of his family to the property—the change of names by the Philistines to obliterate the traces of their origin—the restoration of the names by Isaac, and the contests between the respective shepherds to the exclusive possession of the water, are circumstances that occur amongst the natives in those regions as frequently in the present day as in the time of Isaac."[3]

Another quality in Isaac that merits our emulation was his filial piety, a virtue that has become a casualty in contemporary Western society. He both revered and loved his parents. We may feel that he was a little too submissive to his father for his own good and that it would have been better had he asserted himself more, but it is to his credit that he so fully obeyed the first commandment with a promise.

The Moriah Testing Ground

The first major crisis in Isaac's life was one from which he emerged with flying colors. Would he ever forget that

3. Robert Jamieson, A. R. Faussett, and David Brown, *A Commentary on the Old and New Testaments*, 6 vols. (Grand Rapids: Eerdmans, 1945), vol. 1, *Genesis-Deuteronomy*, by Robert Jamieson, p. 192.

early morning journey up Mount Moriah with his father (Genesis 22)? What a depth of meaning and feeling was concentrated in his poignant question, "Behold, the fire and the wood, but where is the lamb for the burnt offering?" (Genesis 22:7).

The transaction posed a tremendous problem for both Abraham and Isaac, and down through the years, sincere Christians have found in it a puzzling and distressing moral problem. How could God ask such a thing of Abraham? There are some factors involved that go a long way to answering this question.

1. Although God's command confronted Abraham with a traumatic choice that rocked his emotions, it would not have shocked his sensibilities as it would ours today. Human sacrifice was common in that age and society. Such sacrifices were regarded not as crimes, but as acts of worship. Then the father had absolute power of life and death over his son. Such a condition is not confined to ancient times. I once had as a colleague a Bible teacher in Papua, New Guinea, whose father had killed at birth seven of the twelve children born to him—and this is the twentieth century!

2. From the divine side, it is God's method to meet and deal with men on the moral and spiritual level to which they have attained and, through His disciplines, to lift them to higher levels. He accommodates Himself to their stage of growth. Because He sees the end from the beginning, God knew that the sacrificial knife would never be plunged into Isaac's breast. He knew that the issue would not be loss, but immeasurable gain for both Abraham and Isaac—and for the whole world in coming ages. His love is so farseeing that He sacrifices present comfort for eternal profit.

3. Was there any more graphic and effective method God could have adopted to demonstrate the folly and futility of sacrificing "the fruit of the body for the sin of the soul"?

4. An illustration may throw a ray of light on the morality of Abraham's willingness to sacrifice his son. If a servant surreptitiously takes fifty dollars from his employer's till and spends it on himself, he is guilty of a crime. If,

however, his employer tells him to do it, no crime is involved. Although the action is exactly the same in each case, the command of the employer alters its morality.

So, if Abraham had decided on his own initiative to take Isaac's life, he would have been guilty of a crime. But when the deed was done at the command of the Creator, who has absolute authority over the life of His creatures, no crime was involved. In the divine record there is not the slightest indication that Abraham felt any guilt or compunction in obeying God's command, although his own emotions were deeply involved.

5. The incident involved an even greater problem for Isaac than for Abraham, since it was he who was to be the victim. We are not to think of him as a mere lad at the time. He was a mature man of at least twenty-five years of age—the prime of life. A virile young man such as he could very easily have resisted and overcome his centenarian father. This would indicate that he consented to the plan. With characteristic submissiveness he entered into the divine plan in faith, although he must have been as mystified as his father as to how the promise could be fulfilled if he were killed.

This was a tremendous act of self-abnegation for a young man to whom life was just opening out with all it promised for the heir of a wealthy father. The father's example of faith and submission to the will of God had rubbed off on the son, and both emerged from the test with honors.

The Search for a Bride

Isaac remained single until after his mother's death, at which time he was forty years old. Once the mourning rites were completed, Abraham set about obtaining a wife for his son. As the custodian of the divine promise, Isaac was not to marry into the heathen nations, so Abraham sent a trusted servant to his own brother to seek a wife worthy of his son. The story of the servant's successful search for a bride (Genesis 24) is a charming story, a beautiful idyll of love.

So eloquent was the servant in pleading his master's cause that Rebekah lost her heart to Isaac before she saw him. When at last she met Isaac, she alighted from her camel to greet him. When he saw his bride, he must have thought *She is beautiful!* With him it was a case of love at first sight.

Their marriage was subject to the stresses incidental to twenty years of childlessness, a very serious matter in that culture. But God answered Isaac's importunate pleadings and blessed the couple with twin sons. Even before the two brothers' births, the struggle between Esau and Jacob, which struggle was to continue throughout their lives, had begun (Genesis 25:22).

Rebekah was the stronger member of the partnership, and she usually succeeded in outwitting or outmaneuvering her easygoing husband. She had to manage everyone—even God. She could not leave her life and her family in the competent hands of God: she had to manipulate their destinies. To her own sorrow, God allowed her to do it. He still does, and there may be a warning here for the ambitious mother who wants to shape her children after her own image. Rebekah brought endless sorrow on herself and on her loved ones. Esau married two idolatrous Hittite women who never fitted into the family circle; rather, they "brought grief to Isaac and Rebekah" (Genesis 26:34-35).

The Bane of Parental Favoritism

If Christian parents desire to see the tragic outworking of parental favoritism, they need only read this story. Isaac and Rebekah were each drawn to a different son and displayed a foolish partiality. Gentle Isaac was attracted to the uncomplicated, openhearted Esau. Rebekah saw in Jacob's subtle and quieter nature qualities that caused her to favor him. All they succeeded in doing, however, was to lay a trail of bitterness and intrigue that eventually led to a split in the family.

The marriage, which had begun so auspiciously with God's blessing upon it, gradually fell apart. The final pic-

ture is of a lonely and infirm husband being deceived by a
disloyal wife and a scheming son. Had Rebekah realized
that her plot would mean that never again would she see
her favorite son, she would have been slower to enmesh
herself in a web of deceit. Not only did the parents drift
apart, but also the two brothers were trapped in the consequences of their own sin.

Despite some high points, Isaac's career was on the
whole disappointing; his life was characterized by slow
degeneration rather than by steady progress. In early
years he was sacrificial, but in later years he grew self-
indulgent. The sublime faith of his youth became sub-
merged through the years, and it blazed forth in a brief
glow only at the end of life.

Although he reverenced and admired his father, Isaac
did not learn from his father's failures. Like Abraham, he
was guilty of unpardonable disregard of his wife's honor
when he represented to Abimelech that she was his sister
(Genesis 26:1-11). Like his father, too, he was rebuked by
a heathen king who acted more honorably than he did.

A friend once remarked to me, "Isn't it embarrassing to
see your own faults running around on two little legs!"
When Abraham deceived Pharaoh about his wife's identity, he little dreamed that the seeds of his sin would produce a similar sordid harvest in the life of his son.

As a son, Isaac was submissive and affectionate. As a
husband he was devoted, but he abdicated his responsibilities as head of the household. As a father, he was partisan
and indulgent. His place in history is secure, however, for
he is the link between Abraham, the founding father of
the nation, and Jacob, whose posterity from his twelve
sons would constitute the nation. Throughout Scripture
he is ranked as equal with Abraham and Jacob. It is com-
forting to realize that God represents Himself as the God of
the strong man and of the weak man, and even of the
deceitful man.

The Blessing of Jacob

Strangely enough, the event that won Isaac the honor of
a place among the heroes of faith was not some spectacu-

lar achievement, but the fact that "by faith Isaac blessed Jacob and Esau, even regarding things to come [i.e., beyond their lifetime]" (Hebrews 11:20). He thus expressed his faith in the total fulfillment of the promise God had given to his father and had renewed to him (Genesis 26:3). It is a striking fact that as they neared the hour of death, Isaac, Jacob, and Joseph individually expressed in their patriarchal blessings their confidence that although they themselves had not experienced its fulfillment, their descendants would attain greatness in the promised land.

Isaac's faith, which had moved him to costly self-abnegation, flourished again in old age, and that in spite of the deterioration in his character over the years. He contrasted strongly with Caleb. Isaac's request of Esau had been, "Prepare a savory dish for me such as I love" (Genesis 27:4). He might have added, "so that I may indulge my appetite." Caleb's request of Joshua was, "Give me this mountain where the giants are" (cf. Joshua 14:12; and Numbers 13:33). And he might have added, "So that I can conquer them for my God."

Most of us have weak spots in our armor, which weak spots our wily enemy is only too ready to exploit. With old Isaac, food came first and the blessing second (see Genesis 27:4). Alexander Whyte is quoted as saying: "If you would enjoy Isaac's benediction you must get him after his dinner."[4] Sunk in premature senility, he could now be reached only through his senses.

He roused himself from his lethargy to give his blessing to his sons. With prophetic insight and in faith he predicted their careers and those of their descendants. Even in this his faith was faulty, for he sought to circumvent God's declared purpose by trying to pronounce on Esau the blessing God had designed for Jacob. But when he perceived that God had intervened and overruled the deception of Rebekah and Jacob, his faith reasserted itself and he bowed to the sovereign will of God.

When he grasped the full significance of the incident, Isaac refused to withdraw the blessing, even in the face of

4. In Dinsdale T. Young, *Neglected People of the Bible*, 2d ed. (London: Hodder and Stoughton, 1902), p. 18.

the bitter tears of his favorite son. "Yes, and he shall be blessed" was his prophetic declaration (Genesis 27:30-35). Thus out of a failure of faith, faith was reborn.

The early church Fathers, and since then a host of others, saw in Isaac a remarkable type of Christ. His sonship was unique. He was a child of special promise whose birth was predicted long before the event. He was a son of the covenant, and he was his father's heir through whom the promises were to be realized. His conception was not according to the ordinary course of nature. He yielded his life on the altar of sacrifice, thus becoming a suitable type of the Lamb of God. Like Him, he was meek and submissive to his father's will.

4

Job

A Graduate Degree in Suffering

"You have heard of the endurance of Job and have seen the outcome of the Lord's dealings, that the Lord is full of compassion and is merciful" (James 5:11).

There are few among us who know how to minister the comfort of God. Few who know how to *leave their fellows in the hand of God*, and encourage them to "believe their way through" their paths of trial, and still fewer who are able to interpret to stricken hearts the purposes of God in their afflictions.

Knowing little of the inwardness of things, more often do we judge by the sight of the eyes and the hearing of the ears, and come to conclusions from our own standpoint, and according to the measure of our own experience.[1]

(Jessie Penn-Lewis)

An acknowledged literary critic, Richard G. Moulton, once gave it as his opinion that if a jury of persons well instructed in literature were to pronounce which was the greatest poem among the great literatures of the world, the

---

1. Jessie Penn-Lewis, *The Story of Job*, 2d ed. (London: Marshall, 1903), p. 32.

large majority would give their verdict for the book of Job.[2] This great epic poem, so rich in metaphors and similes, is concerned with an Eastern sheikh who was "the greatest of all the men of the east" (Job 1:3).

The book may rightly be termed a theodicy: an attempted vindication of the dealings of God with man. It squarely faces the universal problem of human pain and the mystery of seemingly unmerited suffering. While it does not provide a final answer to the problem, it throws considerable light on the special purpose suffering is intended to serve in the life of the righteous.

The Historicity of Job

Was Job a real historical personage, or was he merely a fictitious character? Until we settle this question, we will be unable to proceed with confidence to interpret the story, which admittedly has some peculiar angles. Some features might well be taken as having symbolical significance; but when the question is objectively faced, the weight of evidence appears to fall on the side of the historicity of the people and events recorded in the book.

The author of the book of Job recounts the circumstantial details in a clear and natural way. His descriptions of Job, his family, and his friends, together with the surrounding details, are presented in a way that would not normally be given in an allegory. The citing of the country he came from and the property he possessed is more in keeping with their being fact than fiction.

That Job was a historical personage has been consistently held by the Jews, who have tenaciously retained the book in their canon of Scripture. Ezekiel associates Job with Noah and Daniel in such a way as to make it illogical not to consider him as much a historical person as the other two (Ezekiel 14:14, 20). James holds him up as an inspiring example of endurance, and includes him among

---

2. In J. Sidlow Baxter, *Explore the Book* (Grand Rapids: Zondervan, 1960), vol. 3, *Poetical Books (Job to Song of Solomon) Isaiah, Jeremiah, Lamentations*, p. 25.

"the prophets who spoke in the name of the Lord" (James 5:10-11). Our Lord quoted from the book (cf. Job 39:30 and Matthew 24:28). Paul also quoted from it, using the formula of inspiration, "It is written" (cf. Job 5:13 and 1 Corinthians 3:19).

The book itself serves a fourfold purpose. (1) As it is perhaps the oldest book of the Old Testament, it gives early insight into the activity of Satan, the archenemy of the race; and, at the same time, it refutes Satan's slander on God's loyal servant Job. (2) It recounts how God through the medium of suffering revealed Job to himself, thus stripping him of the self-righteousness that had limited God's blessing in his life. (3) It grapples with the mystery of suffering. (4) It demonstrates the possibility of a man's maintaining a full consecration to God, even when his whole world is collapsing around his ears.

We are given no account of Job's ancestry, but from the reputed situation of the land of Uz, from which he came, he would be an Arab. Like Melchizedek, he feared the Lord (cf. Job 1:1 and Genesis 14:18-20) and displayed a surprising knowledge of the true God, who did not confine His Self-revelation to the Hebrew race.

The Favorite of God?

Job appears in the story in his mature manhood. In a few terse words, the anonymous author describes his hero as "blameless, upright, fearing God, and turning away from evil" (Job 1:1). His great wealth was in his flocks and herds, the size of which is given in round numbers (Job 1:3). To the Oriental, wealth and prosperity were evidence of the favor of heaven. Light is thrown on the culture of Job's day by references in the book to a knowledge of writing, engraving on stone, mining, metallurgy, astronomy, natural history, and science.

Job's domestic picture is one of relaxed and happy communication and conviviality (Job 1:4). He displayed a deep solicitude for the moral and spiritual welfare of his family. He made regular sacrifices for his children in case they had "sinned and cursed God in their hearts" (Job 1:5). A

happier lot than Job's it would be hard to imagine. But he
has yet to be tested by terrible and unexplained disaster.

The scene was reversed overnight. At one stroke, flocks
and herds, servants and sons and daughters were swept
away (Job 1:13-19). The hour of crisis reveals the true
man. Caught totally unawares, Job reacted like a man
who knows God. "Then Job arose and tore his robe and
shaved his head, and he fell to the ground and worshiped"
(Job 1:20). In the midst of mystery, his sublime faith in
God found expression in the classic affirmation of confidence in God and acceptance of His sovereignty: "The LORD
gave and the LORD has taken away. Blessed be the name of
the LORD" (Job 1:21).

His noble reaction to tragedy won the approval of God
(Job 2:3), but it also aroused the malignity of Satan. One of
the important insights that we gain from the drama that
ensued is that events on earth may have an unsuspected
background in the heavenly realm. Job's relation to the
spirit world and his accessibility to spiritual forces outside
himself are assumed.

There are conflicting views concerning the factuality of
the strange scene presented in Job 1:6-12. Some consider
it to be allegorical, others as actual. A somewhat similar
scene is presented in Zechariah 3:1-5. In Revelation
12:10, Satan again appears as accuser, and as in Job, he
apparently has access to the presence of God. So it is according to the tenor of Scripture to regard the scene as an
actual situation, but expressed in such terms of speech
and action as to make it intelligible to our earth-orientated
minds.

A Glimpse of a Heavenly Council

For a brief moment the curtain is drawn aside, and we
are permitted a glimpse into the court of heaven. It was in
this gathering that Job's crescendo of trial had its origin,
but God kindly veiled his eyes to that fact. Had he been
granted a vision of its heavenly background before the
blows fell, his faith would have had no opportunity of soar-

ing to the heights it ultimately attained. The epilogue must not be written before the prologue.

It was audience day in the court of heaven. Among those who had come to make their report to the throne was Satan, the adversary, who apparently had some official right to be present. Asked where he came from, he replied, "From roaming about on the earth and walking around on it" (Job 1:7). The nature of his activities can be judged by the fact that the Hebrew word for "roaming" here signifies "roaming about as a spy." Milton described him accurately when he called him "sabbathless Satan."

Jehovah put a question to Satan: "Have you considered [set your heart on] My servant Job? For there is no one like him on the earth, a blameless and upright man, fearing God and turning away for evil" (Job 1:8). Coming as it did from the omniscient God, this is an amazing eulogy. We must, however, guard against reading full New Testament meaning into the word "perfect," which appears in the King James Version. It carries the idea of completeness, not of sinlessness. "Blameless" is the preferable translation. It means that he was a man of mature, well-rounded character.

True to his nature, Satan made a sneering rejoinder. He had the effrontery to suggest that God was naive to suppose that Job's piety was disinterested. Job was loyal to God, but only because of the benefits he received from Him. In any case, Satan alleged, God had put a hedge of privilege around him (Job 1:9-11). "Withdraw the blessings, and he will curse You to Your face." Thus Satan threw down the gauntlet.

God accepted the challenge, removed the hedge, and gave Satan permission to put Job to the test, but within strictly prescribed limits (Job 1:12). Calamity after calamity overwhelmed Job. As a result of satanic activity, he lost his wealth through marauders and freak storms. Then he lost his whole family—seven sons and three daughters at a stroke. Though he was brokenhearted and devastated, "through all this Job did not sin nor did he blame God" (Job 1:22). Satan had lost the first round, but he had other tricks in his bag.

The Outcast on the Ash Heap

Once again came audience day at the court of heaven. Unabashed by his crushing defeat, Satan again presented himself. Once again God asserted His confidence in Job's integrity and altruism. Once again Satan sneered: "Just give me permission to rack his body with pain and see if he does not renounce his loyalty." Mysteriously to us, God granted the permission, but with the stipulation that Job's life must be spared (Job 2:6).

Satan struck Job with disease. The nature of the loathsome affliction with which he was stricken is not certain. It may have been a virulent and repulsive form of leprosy, or it may have been elephantiasis. In any case, it was sufficiently serious and offensive for his fellow citizens to banish him from the city, and he sat among the ashes outside the gate (Job 2:8). So unbearable was the suffering that he longed for nothing more than death.

From being "the greatest of all men of the east," Job had become an outcast on the dunghill. Such was the malignity of Satan toward the holiest man of his age. From the purely human angle, there seemed justification for Job's wife's bitter jibe: "Do you still hold fast your integrity? Curse God and die" (Job 2:9).

The greatness of the man shines through his noble reply: " 'You speak as one of the foolish women speaks. Shall we indeed accept good from God and not accept adversity?' *In all this Job did not sin with his lips*" (Job 2:10, italics added). Satan had lost the second round. Job had proved to God, man, and devil a complete absence of self-interest in his devotion to God. He loved God for His own sake, and not for the blessings He bestowed. Francis Xavier might have had Job in mind when he penned these words:

> My God, I love Thee; not because
>   I hope for heaven thereby,
> Not yet because who love Thee not
> Are lost eternally.
> . . . .
> Not from the hope of gaining aught,

> Not seeking a reward;
> But as Thyself hast lovèd me,
> O ever-loving Lord.

Thus Job demonstrated his genuine loyalty and love for God first in undisturbed prosperity, then in unrelieved adversity, and finally in his triumphant affirmation "Though He slay me, I will hope in Him" (Job 13:15).

The Strategy of Satan

Job's experience throws valuable light on the nature of our satanic foe and the strategy he employs. The very methods he used then to seduce men from allegiance to God, he employs today.

(1) Job's mystifying sufferings are explained in part by the fact that, all unknown to him, he was a battlefield on which a contest between God and Satan was being fought. God had staked everything on Job's integrity, and Satan was using every weapon at his disposal to shatter Job's confidence in God. (2) The initiative in the conflict lay not with Satan, but with God, who saw through Satan's malicious plan. (3) Any power Satan possesses is not inherent, but delegated. He is a creature and is neither omniscient nor omnipotent. (4) Satan does not have unrestricted liberty; rather, he is accountable to God for his actions. His power is limited to what God permits. (5) Satan has no counterweapon to the shield of faith.

There is much comfort for the hard-pressed soul in these revealed facts. Satan has no more power to cause us pain and loss than God in His love and wisdom permits (Job 1:12; 2:6). God will never allow affliction and testing greater than we are able to bear (1 Corinthians 10:13). When for some adequate but unexplained reason God does bring us into severe testing, He always makes available additional and sufficient grace (2 Corinthians 12:9).

The very fact that some of God's mysterious dealings with us are not explained is often a cause of distress. "I could bear it, if only I knew why!" we cry. In this context G. Campbell Morgan has this to say: "There are many who do not know the ultimate meaning of the experiences through which they are passing to-day. They are hidden away, with some suffering, some agony, some trouble gripping their hearts; not the result of their own sin. They say, What is God doing? I cannot tell them. But this book suggests that there is a meaning, and there is a value. . . . I think it is fair speculation, that Job, in the life beyond, will be thanking God for all he passed through."[3] Like Job, we can learn that suffering has other and higher functions than penalty.

Job's trials were not yet over. He had lost possessions, family, health, and the support of his wife. What was left? He still had an honored name among his friends and contemporaries, and he was now attacked by his friends on this point.

Job's Comforters

Through the desert grapevine, Eliphaz, Bildad, Zophar, and Elihu learned of Job's distress, and with genuine concern and sympathy they came to comfort their friend. So terrible was the transformation caused by his sufferings that they did not recognize him (Job 2:12). They are often referred to disparagingly as "Job's comforters," and in some ways they merit this stricture. But before we condemn them out of hand, we must remember that while his other friends stood aloof when tragedy overwhelmed him, they came to be with him in his suffering. They came and sat with him in silent sympathy for seven days. Although they said some devastating things about him, at least they did not say them behind his back.

The prologue (Job 1-2) is followed by one of the most moving and pathetic monologues in literature (Job 3). When Job broke the seven days of silence, it was to pour out the bitterness of his heart. One cannot read it and enter into his mood without being deeply affected. "Let the day perish on which I was to be born. . . . Why did I not die

3. G. Campbell Morgan, *The Answers of Jesus to Job* (New York: Revell, 1935), pp. 19-20.

at birth? . . . Why is . . . life [given] to the bitter of soul?"
(Job 3:3, 11, 20).

These were petulant words, but they were squeezed out
of him. There is therapeutic value in giving expression to
our bewilderment, provided it does not lead us to impugn
God's love or wisdom. Note that while Job cursed his day,
he did not curse his God, as Satan was inciting him to do.

The remainder of the book is occupied with the three
rounds of dialogue between Job and his friends. In reading
these remarkable orations, we should bear in mind that
while the inspired author gives us an accurate account of
the dialogue, that fact does not automatically invest with
truth all that the men said. Much was indeed true, but the
point is that although it was true, it was not always appli-
cable to Job's case. The right principles were applied to
the wrong person.

The friends contended that it is only the wicked who
suffer. If a man finds himself greatly afflicted, it is because
he has sinned greatly. In *the first round* (Job 4-14), Eliphaz insisted that God blesses the just and punishes the
unjust. The inference is obvious. Bildad and Zophar followed the same line of reasoning and urged Job to repent
of his sin. Job resisted their imputations and appealed to
God to vindicate his integrity. He showed how it is often
the wicked who prosper and that God acts sovereignly and
without respect of persons.

In *round two* (Job 15-21), their condolence turned into
condemnation. Job had to be hypocritically concealing
some great sin, for it is the wicked alone who suffer. Again
Job refuted their arguments, proving that the wicked often
prosper and are full of years and flinging back their baseless insinuations. It is in this debate that Job made his
peerless confession: "I know that my Redeemer lives, and
at the last He will take His stand on the earth. Even after
my skin is destroyed, yet from my flesh I shall see God;
whom I myself shall behold, and whom my eyes shall see
and not another" (Job 19:25-27).

The third round (Job 22-31) saw the philosophers relentlessly pursuing their attack on the embattled Job. Reasoning gave place to accusation and sarcasm. Job again

passionately protested his innocence, and the debate came
to an indecisive end. The four friends had been wrong in
maintaining that God had acted *retributively,* but Job was
equally wrong in suggesting that He had acted *arbitrarily*
and without adequate reason. He had not yet mastered the
fundamental lesson that there was nothing in him to de-
serve God's favor, and he was still stubbornly justifying
himself to them.

Job's Afflictions Are Chastisements

Then Elihu took up the cudgels (Job 32-37). As a younger man, he had deferred to seniority, but he now summed
up the previous discussion: "The anger of Elihu . . .
burned; against Job his anger burned, because he justified
himself before God. And his anger burned against his
three friends because they had found no answer, and yet
had condemned Job" (Job 32:2-3).

In his long oration, he showed keener insight than his
elders. God's afflictions are not judgemnts, as they had
maintained, but chastisements, sent to restrain men from
the proud attitude that leads to the pit (Job 33:17). Thus
affliction has its origin not in retribution, but in the tender
love of God, with the end in view that man might "be
enlightened with the light of life" (Job 33:30). He appealed
to Job to recognize his own ignorance and impotence and
show humility instead of self-righteousness. Instead of demanding explanations of God, he should exercise faith and
patience.

At this point Jehovah Himself dramatically intervened
and spoke out of a whirlwind (Job 38-42). In the presence
of the divine majesty, the whole group was reduced to silence. God gave no simplistic answer to the problem under
discussion, but He posed a mounting series of questions
that demolished Job's fancied goodness and banished his
misconceptions of God and His dealings. Job was made to
see that since he was so profoundly ignorant even of God's
activities in nature, how much more ignorant he had to be
in the realm of God's moral government in the world. At

last he saw that God's chastening is designed to bring men first to self-despair and then to unquestioning confidence in a God who cares and can be trusted.

It was the majestic vision of God that brought Job to his knees in contrition and worship—the point to which God had all the time been moving. Humbly now Job made his confession: "I know that Thou canst do all things, and that no purpose of Thine can be thwarted. . . . Therefore I have declared that which I did not understand, things too wonderful for me, which I did not know. . . . I have heard of Thee by the hearing of the ear; but now my eye sees Thee; therefore I retract, and I repent in dust and ashes" (Job 42:2-6).

Job had graduated from the school of suffering. Egotism had evaporated. Humility ousted pride. Patience could now have her perfect work.

The saga closed with Job vindicated by God before his friends and Satan and blessed with double of what he had before. "And the LORD blessed the latter days of Job more than his beginning" (Job 42:12). We see him in the role of intercessor for his friends whose mistaken strictures had more nearly caused him to stumble than Satan's fiery darts. His fortunes were restored when he prayed for his critical friends (Job 42:10). Is there a lesson for us in this?

The gift from God of seven more sons and three more daughters throws an incidental sidelight on the Bible doctrine of immortality. God increased all Job's material possessions twofold, but what about his family? In addition to his ten living children, ten were awaiting him on the other side. Job was seventy when his troubles overtook him, and God gave him seventy more years in which to enjoy the harvest from his trials.

> By sufferings only can we know
>   The nature of the life we live;
> The temper of our souls they show,
>   How true, how pure, the love we give.
> To leave my love in doubt would be
> No less disgrace than misery.

I welcome then with heart sincere,
    The cross my Saviour bids me take;
No load, no trial is severe,
    That's borne or suffered for His sake:
And thus my sorrow shall proclaim
A love that's worthy of the name.

                    (Jeanne Marie de la Mothe Guyon)

5

Rahab

The Romance of the Scarlet Cord

"In the same way was not Rahab the harlot also justified by works, when she received the messengers and sent them out by another way?" (James 2:25).

The story of Rahab is strangely interwoven with the victory of Joshua. The book that tells us of the highest Christian life quickly reminds us of the mercy of God for the vilest sinner, and bids us blend the work of salvation with the higher work of sanctification. The heart of God is as much concerned in seeking and saving the lost as in leading His people into a higher blessing.[1]

(A. B. Simpson)

Where else but in the Bible would one expect to find such an odd conjunction of names as these? "The book of the genealogy of Jesus Christ. . . . Abraham . . . Isaac . . . Jacob . . . Rahab" (Matthew 1:1-2, 5). "By faith Rahab the harlot . . . Gideon . . . David and Samuel" (Hebrews 11:31-32).

Who but God would select as a progenitor of His Son a

1. A. B. Simpson, *The Epistle to the Hebrews* (Harrisburg, Pa.: Christian Publications, n.d.), pp. 81-82.

Canaanite woman who was not only outside the Hebrew covenant, but also outside the pale of decent society? How remarkable that one of the only two women to find their way into the illustrious company of Hebrews 11 should be this woman! And how remarkable that she should be one of the four women included in the genealogy of the Messiah. It is an example of the glorious universality of God's grace. These facts, too, mark Rahab out as a woman of more than passing importance in the religious history of the world.

Many have ventured, from honorable motives, to remove the stigma from this ancestress of the Lord by toning down the harsh Hebrew word for "harlot" and making it mean something more in the nature of a hostess in a tavern. But the attempt lacks any satisfactory basis. Scriptural usage, supported by the Septuagint version and followed by the apostles, establishes the traditional meaning of the word "harlot." Further, Eastern taverns or khans were never kept by women.

The environment in which Rahab lived made it very difficult for a young woman to retain her virtue. This makes her faith and subsequent career the more remarkable, for she was the only person in Jericho to so respond. The citizens of Jericho were cruel, idolatrous demon-worshipers, and it was for this reason that God had commanded their destruction.

From the Ras Shamra Tablets we learn that among the deities they worshiped were the gods of fertility, Baal and Ashtaroth, whose worship encouraged sexual license. Chemosh, a god to whom child sacrifices were offered, was also in their pantheon. The wonder is not so much that Rahab became a harlot as that she responded so readily to the call of God. She was a glowing example of the fact that faith can flourish in a most inhospitable environment.

The Courage of Faith

Joshua, whom God had charged to be the instrument of divine retribution on Jericho, sent two men secretly to reconnoiter. All unconscious that they had been spotted by the sentries, they entered the city and sought lodging. Was it by chance or by divine overruling that they were directed to the house of Rahab? It had probably been recommended to them because of its convenient situation on the city wall, and they were not necessarily aware of its unsavory reputation.

To offer hospitality to two total strangers whose identity she had guessed was a courageous act on Rahab's part. But it was also an act of treason for which she could expect no mercy if discovered. Behind her action there was strong motivation. From her testimony (Joshua 2:9-11), it is clear that the inhabitants of Canaan and Jericho were well informed about the victories God had given Israel, and they were desperately afraid (Joshua 2:24). Rahab herself shared in the fear: "I know," she confessed, "that the LORD has given you the land, and that the terror of you has fallen on us" (Joshua 2:9).

A glimmer of faith had dawned in Rahab's heart, and she now realized that God was offering her an alternative. At risk of her life she offered the men hospitality, even going so far as to conceal them from the police. Furthermore, she told a lie in order to protect them. She could tell that these men were different from those she normally entertained. Sensing that this was a heaven-sent opportunity to change sides, she made up her mind to switch her allegiance and identify herself with Israel and Israel's God.

Is a Lie Ever Justified?

Was Rahab justified in telling a lie, even in such a good cause? This is an often debated question. May there be cases in which the end justifies the means? We must acknowledge that she was an exemplary character neither morally nor ethically, but we should not judge her actions in terms of our own enlightened standards. We live in the full blaze of the sun. She lived in the dawn.

Lying is so universal a vice among pagan peoples that Rahab would have had no compunction and felt no guilt for her deceit. Indeed, she would have felt guilt had she not done as she did. In Oriental ethics, to protect one's guest is regarded as one of the highest virtues. Eastern hospitality requires a man to preserve the life even of his bitterest enemy—if he has eaten of his salt.

But the ethical question still remains to be answered. From the scriptural view, lying is always sin, and it is said to be something that must be put away. "Laying aside falsehood," said Paul, "speak truth, each one of you, with his neighbor" (Ephesians 4:25). There are no degrees of truth. God nowhere suggests or implies that the end justifies the means.

Did God condone and approve Rahab's lie? There is nothing in the record to imply that He did. He did not need Rahab to lie on His behalf in order to protect His servants. He could have done it in a dozen other ways. God never resorts to or condones a sinful expedient. James does not commend her for her deception when he says, "In the same way was not Rahab the harlot also justified by works, when she received the messengers and sent them out by another way?" (James 2:25). It was her brave and unselfish act and her faith that he commended, not her lying.

That she was a clever and resourceful woman is seen in the subtle ruse she devised to conceal the spies from detection. Perhaps this was not the first time she had sheltered some of her clients from the police! But despite the kind of life she had lived, deep in her heart was the desire for something better. And God met her on that ground.

Heaven's Kindly Judgment

In His judgment of sinful men and women, Jesus takes every factor into account. When the wily scribes and Pharisees brought to him a woman caught in the act of adultery, Jesus asked her, " 'Did no one condemn you?' And she said, 'No one, Lord.' And Jesus said, 'Neither do I condemn you; go your way; from now on sin no more' " (John 8:10-11). He knows, as William Booth so graphically put it, that many helpless children are not born into the world, but are damned into the world, while most of us are hedged about with privilege, and He takes these factors into account.

It was the realization that while God does not condone sin, He does have a compassionate heart for sinning men and women, that moved F. W. Faber to write:

> There's a wideness in God's mercy,
> Like the wideness of the sea;
> There's a kindness in His justice,
> Which is more than liberty.
>
> . . . .
>
> For the love of God is broader
> Than the measure of man's mind;
> And the heart of the Eternal
> Is most wonderfully kind.

It took no small degree of moral courage on Rahab's part to take a lone stand among her people by embracing the religion of the hated and feared Israelites. But so profound was the impression made on her by the miracle at the Red Sea and the rout of the mighty Amorite kings Sihon and Og, that while it struck terror into her heart, it also kindled a spark of faith. Then as now, faith comes by hearing. She heard and tremblingly believed. Her faith was born of the supernatural evidence she had seen in the experience of God's people, and so she transferred her allegiance to their God.

Convinced as she was that Jericho was to be destroyed by the Israelites, Rahab determined that if there was any possibility of being delivered, she would not be saved alone. When the spies promised her immunity from the impending judgment (Joshua 2:14), her thoughts immediately flew to her family, and she interceded on their behalf. It takes no vivid imagination to picture her going about the city warning her relatives of the coming holocaust and importuning them to share the shelter of her hospitable roof. In this noble feature of her character she puts many Christians to shame. She was not content to "eat her morsel, herself, alone" (cf. Job 31:17).

Faith Seen in Deeds

The outstanding feature of Rahab's character was her faith in a newly discovered God. This secured for a dissolute Gentile woman not only a place among His people, but a place of honor alongside the great heroes of that nation—Abraham, Moses, and David. God values faith highly; so highly, indeed, that it is impossible to please Him without it (Hebrews 11:6).

Her progress in the life of faith was simple and rapid. She heard of the mighty works of God and believed. "I know that the LORD has given you the land" was her astounding confession (Joshua 2:9). Where had she obtained her knowledge? Where there is a seeking soul, there is also a seeking God. The Holy Spirit enlightened her responsive heart and mind to see who the true God was. "The LORD your God, He is God in heaven above and on earth beneath" (Joshua 2:11). It is a solemnizing truth that the same evidence that created faith in Rahab's heart only hardened the resistance of her fellow citizens.

James asserted that Rahab showed her faith by her deeds (James 2:25), for faith provides the motivation for obedience. Before she helped the men escape down the wall, she obtained from them the promise that she and all in her house would be spared. But the promise was conditional. (1) Safety would be guaranteed only to those who remained in the house (Joshua 2:19). (2) An identifying scarlet cord had to be bound in the window (Joshua 2:18). (3) The mission of the spies had to be kept secret. In the event, the conditions were fulfilled, and all in Rahab's house were spared.

Many expositors have seen in this incident a deeper significance than appears on the surface. It is very possible to carry the allegorization of Scripture to absurd limits. But there is sound New Testament warrant for seeing a spiritual significance in certain Old Testament facts and incidents.

"Sir William Robertson Nicoll has said that the words of the Old Testament are strangely prepared to hold the glory of the New," wrote W. H. Parker. "The intense utterances on life and death scattered through the Old Testament have another meaning for those who have heard the Lord saying, 'he that believeth in Me shall never die.'

"And so in the New Testament we find this narrative of

Rahab illumined, new meanings uncovered, the whole story shining with gospel truth. For 'all these things happened unto them for examples: and they are written for our admonition upon whom the ends of the ages are come' " (cf. 1 Corinthians 10:11).[2]

It will be remembered that Jesus did not hesitate to draw unexpected lessons from Old Testament incidents such as Moses' lifting of the brazen serpent (John 3:14). Behind the symbol was a fact. With such spiritual precedents, we venture to draw some lessons from the binding of the scarlet cord in the window of Rahab's house, which act insured its inmates of immunity from destruction.

An Interesting Parallel

There is an interesting parallel between some features of the Passover and this incident. In the Passover observance, the prohibition was "None of you shall go outside the door of his house until morning" (Exodus 12:22). In this case the condition was, "Anyone who goes out of the doors of your house into the street, his blood shall be on his own head, and we shall be free" (Joshua 2:19). Safety from impending judgment, in both cases, depended on remaining under the shelter of the specially marked house. At the Passover, crimson blood was splashed on the door. In Rahab's case, a scarlet cord was bound in the window. When God saw the blood, He passed over them as He promised. When Joshua saw the scarlet cord, the house and its inmates were divinely protected from destruction as promised. In the two symbols it is not difficult to see the redemption and salvation from judgment procured by the blood of the cross and personally appropriated.

What significance can be seen in the scarlet cord? (1) Rahab and her family had now chosen to identify themselves with the God of Israel and His people. (2) All who sheltered in the house were equally under the protection of God. (3) Each had taken this step of faith individ-

2. W. H. Parker, "A Study in Scarlet," *The Evangelical Christian*, March 1942, p. 102.

ually and voluntarily. (4) They were immune from divine judgment. Just as the Hebrew families could eat the Passover feast in perfect safety behind the blood-sprinkled door, so the little company gathered in Rahab's house could wait for deliverance in perfect confidence and without fear behind the scarlet cord. (5) Rahab was now included in the covenant of promise and was thus eligible to become a progenitor of the Jewish Messiah.

Who could have dreamed such a denouement to such a sordid story? The harlot's house becomes a house of prayer. The harlot herself becomes the ancestress of David, king and sweet psalmist of Israel, and greater still, of Jesus Christ, Son of Man and Son of God.

6

Ruth

An Unorthodox Courtship

*"Where you go, I will go. . . . Your people shall be my
people, and your God, my God"* (Ruth 1:16).

One of the most beautiful stories in the Bible is the story of
Ruth. Here we have what the world is never weary of listening to, a true love-story. And the fact that the heroine is a
young widow does not in the least detract from the glamour
of the story. For what could be more appealing than the ad-
venturous and romantic experience of the young woman,
who finds happiness after having plumbed the depths of sorrow and of loss?[1]

(Donald Davidson)

The book of Ruth is a prose idyll that is to be measured
by its beauty, not its bulk. It is exquisite in its simplicity,
and it affords welcome relief from the violence and law-
lessness of the book of Judges, which precedes it. In this
little biographical interlude, the curtain of contemporary
domestic life is drawn back to reveal that the gentler
graces and virtues had not altogether disappeared from
the life of apostate Israel.

1. Donald Davidson, *Mothers in the Bible* (London: Marshall, Morgan &
   Scott, 1934), p. 62.

Ruth's story begins at Bethlehem with a famine that resulted in the emigration to Moab of Elimelech, his wife Naomi, and their two sons, Mahlon and Chilion. But emigration does not necessarily secure exemption from further trouble. First Elimelech died, and the sons married Moabite women. Then they too died, leaving Ruth and Orpah as widows. An endemic malaria especially virulent among males was a scourge in that area, and it is likely that it was the cause of the deaths of the three men.

Naomi was left in a foreign land, a widow with two dependent and widowed daughters-in-law. The famine was severe throughout the land, and not until ten years had elapsed did it abate. When Naomi heard that "the Lord had visited His people in giving them food" (Ruth 1:6), she decided to return to her own land and home. With breaking heart, she unselfishly urged her daughters to remain with their people. In their distress and indecision, the three weeping widows must have presented an affecting sight.

Orpah yielded to her mother's persuasion, but Ruth refused to leave Naomi and clung to her. Her response to Naomi's gentle pressure is unusually fine: "Ruth said, 'Do not urge me to leave you or turn back from following you; for where you go, I will go, and where you lodge, I will lodge. Your people shall be my people, and your God, my God. Where you die, I will die, and there I will be buried. Thus may the Lord do to me, and worse, if anything but death parts you and me' " (Ruth 1:16-17).

"Her vow has stamped itself on the very heart of the world," wrote Samuel Cox. "And that not because of the beauty of its form simply, though even in our English version it sounds like a sweet and noble music, but because it expresses in a worthy form, and once for all, the utter devotion of a genuine and self-conquering love."[2]

Ruth's Confession of Faith

Ruth's choice of Naomi's God in preference to her own gods was her confession of faith. She had been impressed

---

2. In W. G. Moorehead, *Outline Studies in the Old Testament* (1893; reprint ed., Grand Rapids: Zondervan, n.d.), pp. 83-84.

by the contrast between her cruel god, Chemosh, and the merciful God of Israel. She liked what she saw of Jehovah as manifested in the life of Naomi and her family. She was first won to Naomi, and then through her, to Naomi's God. Naomi must have been a noble woman to win such affection from her daughter-in-law.

Orpah apparently was not so deeply impressed with Jehovah as was Ruth, and when the choice came, she returned to her gods (Ruth 1:15). Unlike Orpah, when Ruth was confronted with the choice of the higher and a lower road, she chose the higher, and with saddened steps the two widows traversed it back to Bethlehem.

Ruth's was not an easy and costless decision. So far as she knew, she was electing for a life of poverty among strangers. Not only that, she was a Moabitess, and Moabites were anathema to the Jews. So she could expect ostracism and hostility. Since Orpah had returned, Ruth would have no congenial company of her own age and race. In Moab there would be the possibility of a husband, but not in Israel. Ruth's decision was thus a sincere expression of her deep and genuine love for both Naomi and her God.

As they drew near Bethlehem, "all the city was stirred because of them" (Ruth 1:19). Memories of former times crowded in on Naomi, and she greeted her old friends with the pathetic cry, "Do not call me Naomi [sweet]; call me Mara [bitter], for the Almighty has dealt very bitterly with me. I went out full, but the LORD has brought me back empty" (Ruth 1:20-21). The succession of calamities had caused her faith to go into eclipse. In flying from one trouble, she had encountered something worse; for to her, death was a sign of divine disapproval.

Divine Providence

The two widows had to earn a living, for they had been met with more curiosity than sympathy, and no tangible offers of help had been received. So, as a dutiful and loving daughter, Ruth assumed responsibility for the support of the home.

In the company of the Jewish maidens, she went out to

glean in the barley fields. There is a lovely touch about
what followed. "She happened to come" to the portion of
the field belonging to Boaz (Ruth 2:3). And who did Boaz
happen to be? "Now Naomi had a kinsman of her husband,
a man of great wealth, of the family of Elimelech, whose
name was Boaz" (Ruth 2:1). Boaz was a gentleman farmer
who was none other than the son of Rahab the harlot, who
had been so wonderfully delivered from the destruction of
Jericho (Matthew 1:5). So, in this timely provision for two
needy widows, we see God's providence at work. He overruled tragedy for blessing, and He revealed Himself as a
God of grace and mercy.

The field in which they were gleaning, although a large
undivided area, was made up of the aggregate portions of
land owned by the inhabitants of the town. This makes it
the more remarkable that it was in Boaz's portion she first
came to glean. In the reciprocal greetings that passed between Boaz and his reapers, there is a pleasing picture of
simple Oriental life.

To Boaz's "May the LORD be with you," the reapers responded, "May the LORD bless you" (Ruth 2:4). To Boaz and
the reapers, the salutation was not an empty form, but an
acknowledgment of the Lord and the expression of a desire
for the welfare of each other. Before they had degenerated
into a sterile formality, such as our *good-bye* (a contrac-
tion of "God be with you"), such salutations were really
prayers for those addressed.

The Mosaic law held a charitable provision for people
who found themselves in Ruth's unenviable position. It
runs: "Now when you reap the harvest of your land, you
shall not reap to the very corners of your field, neither
shall you gather the gleanings of your harvest. . . . You
shall leave them for the needy and for the stranger. I am
the LORD your God" (Leviticus 19:9-10). Ruth benefited under this provision.

It might be asked, How was Ruth, a Moabitess, able to
make herself intelligible to the servant in charge of the
reaping (Ruth 2:6-7)? The answer is that an inscription
found on the Moabite stone discovered in 1868 proves that
there was very little difference between the Moabitish and

the Hebrew languages—much as is the case in the differences of dialect in England or America.

When Boaz heard the story of Ruth's self-sacrifice and love for Naomi, he was moved to do something to alleviate her lot. He urged her not to go into any other fields to glean, but to stay with his maids. He also quietly passed the word to the reapers to drop as if by accident a few sheaves for her to glean. Her courtesy, humility, and gratitude were not lost on Boaz, who extended special favors to her (Ruth 2:14) and gave instruction that she was not to be subjected to any insult.

Levirate Marriage

For a full understanding of the story, it is necessary to know the background of levirate marriage, that is, the law of near of kin, expressed in Deuteronomy 25:5-6. (Matthew 22:23-30 is based on this concept of levirate marriage.) It provides that "when brothers live together and one of them dies and has no son, the wife of the deceased shall not be married outside the family to a strange man. Her husband's brother shall go in to her and take her to himself as wife and perform the duty of a husband's brother to her. And it shall be that the firstborn whom she bears shall assume the name of his dead brother, that his name may not be blotted out from Israel."

This provision had a threefold purpose: (1) to preserve posterity, (2) to protect the inheritance, and (3) to save from poverty. In the case of Naomi and Ruth, all three ends were secured.

Naomi had a kinsman who was nearer to her than Boaz, but he was unwilling to redeem her inheritance from her late husband's estate. The course of action that Naomi counseled Ruth to follow in these circumstances (see Ruth 3:1-4) was really an indirect plea to Boaz to undertake the kinsman-redeemer duties that her nearer relative had refused to assume.

Her strategy may sound strange and immodest to our ears, but she was not being bold or forward in acting as she did. It was recognized Jewish practice, and it carried no immoral implications. Our Western method in such an event would probably be to present a strong case to Boaz for his undertaking the responsibility, but Oriental peoples prefer a symbolic act, and that is what Naomi suggested.

Boaz responded with tact and true nobility of character to this delicate situation. He had been much drawn to the attractive young Moabitess, so he promised that if the near kinsman failed in his duty, he would redeem both her and the property (Ruth 3:13). The whole incident was conducted with propriety (Ruth 3:14), and he proved as good as his word. When Ruth returned in the morning with six ephahs of barley, Naomi knew that her strategy had paid off and that all she had to do now was to await the peal of the wedding bells.

The story of the redemption is told in elaborate detail in Ruth 4. The total redemption price included not only the mortgaged land, but also Ruth herself. "You must also acquire Ruth the Moabitess, the widow of the deceased, in order to raise up the name of the deceased on his inheritance" (Ruth 4:5). Apparently, the near kinsman was not sufficiently wealthy both to redeem the land for Ruth's heir and to support Ruth and her family without jeopardizing his own land (Ruth 4:6); so we must not judge him too harshly. In the end, it was Boaz who purchased the alienated land and redeemed the person of Ruth (Ruth 4:9-10).

A sanctified imagination will have little difficulty in seeing in the action of Boaz a picture of our Kinsman Redeemer, who buys us back to Himself and redeems our alienated inheritance (see 1 Corinthians 6:19-20; 1 Peter 1:3-5). Like Boaz, our Redeemer not only restores the forefeited inheritance, but also gives Himself to His bride.

The charming story has important and, indeed, universal overtones. It supplies an important link in the genealogy of David, and therefore in that of David's greater Son, for Boaz was David's grandfather. It foreshadows the New Testament truth that Gentiles are fellow heirs with Jews (Ephesians 3:6). It gives a heartwarming insight into ideal relations between mother-in-law and daughter-in-law. It provides a delightful true love story.

Ruth's sacrificial decision brought her not only sustenance, but also a loving husband; and it introduced her into the very line from which the Messiah would come. Thus she became a focus of blessing to the world in succeeding ages.

What tremendous and unsuspected issues might hang on a single decision! How important, then, that depending on God to guide us, we make the right ones.

7

Jephthah

An Eastern Robin Hood

"Jephthah the Gileadite was a valiant warrior . . . and Jephthah made a vow to the LORD" (Judges 11:1, 30).

> Vows are very unfashionable to-day. . . . This is an age when moral commitments and pledges to God are seldom asked for. So low is the condition of modern Christendom that . . . vows are broken; they are broken in marriage now more freely than ever in the history of our country. They are broken between the nations with impunity.[1]
>
> (T. M. Bamber)

What relevance can Christians who live in the space age find in the life of an obscure Eastern Robin Hood? One answer is that "all Scripture is inspired by God and profitable for teaching, for reproof, for correction, for training in righteousness; that the man of God may be adequate, equipped for every good work" (2 Timothy 3:16-17).

The story of Jephthah has been included in Scripture for this purpose. It is axiomatic that anyone whose name is found inscribed on God's honors list is someone of more

---

1. T. M. Bamber, "Jepthah's Vow," in *The Keswick Convention: 1939* (London: Pickering & Inglis, n.d.), p. 73.

than ordinary caliber (Hebrews 11:32). Those who qualified for this investiture were, without exception, distinguished graduates in the school of faith. It was by faith that Jephthah "conquered kingdoms, . . . became mighty in war, put foreign armies to flight" (Hebrews 11:33-34). This alone is sufficient to warrant research into the qualities that singled him out for such high honor.

Jephthah, the son of Gilead and an Aramean woman, was the ninth Judge of Israel, and he controlled the destiny of that nation for six years. His mother was a harlot. Born under unfavorable conditions, the son of a secondary wife, he had an inferior status in the family and shared the stigma that rested on his mother. Because of his illegitimacy, his brothers would not recognize him as a member of the clan. When he reached manhood, they disinherited him and drove him from their home.

He fled to Tob, probably to the home of his mother's people. There he gathered around him, much as King David did in later years, a band of "worthless fellows" (Judges 11:3)—probably unemployed. There is no necessary implication that they were vicious, but they were probably wild and reckless and lived as outlaws. Jephthah welded them into an effective fighting force; and as their leader, he earned the reputation of a mighty man of valor. They doubtless made frequent incursions into Ammonite territory, but in those lawless days such activities were not considered dishonest, provided the people attacked were outside one's own tribe.

In our age, in which the institution of marriage is increasingly threatened and the number of illegitimate births is burgeoning, the innocent victims of the prevalent promiscuity should not be reproached or disadvantaged only because of the hereditary misfortune over which they had no control. The sin was that of the parents, and any reproach should be theirs. There are comfort and encouragement for any who are innocently suffering as the result of the lax morals of our society in the fact that Jephthah's heredity did not permanently affect his career, for he became the honored leader of his nation. Nor did it exclude him from being highly honored by God.

The fact that his own parents never married caused great grief and distress to Scotland's celebrated preacher Alexander Whyte. But although it clouded his life, the sorrow exercised a mellowing influence on his rugged character and imparted a singularly moving note to his preaching.

God's Way Up Is Down

God similarly overruled the tragedy of the circumstances of Jephthah's birth. Like Joseph, had his brothers not repudiated him he might never have become the first man of his nation. It was during his banishment that he developed the skill in war that won him his leadership. Joseph's words to his brothers would have been equally appropriate on Jephthah's lips: "As for you, you meant evil against me, but God meant it for good in order to bring about this present result" (Genesis 50:20). God has His own training methods, and it is usually true that His way up first leads down, for the mountain is only as high as the valley is deep.

An acute crisis arose when the Ammonites threatened Jephthah's countrymen, the Gileadites, with invasion. The crisis does not always make the man, but it usually reveals what is in him. It certainly did so for Gilead's rejected son.

The Gileadites were lacking in leadership, and in their extremity they turned to the man they had repudiated. He had proved himself a competent warrior, and his band of trained and daring men would be a great asset in any engagement. It would appear that some of Jephthah's brothers were in the deputation (Judges 11:7). In view of their callous treatment of him, he doubtless felt justified in being a bit dramatic.

"Did you not hate me and drive me from my father's house?" he asked. "So why have you come to me now when you are in trouble?" (Judges 11:7). But being a true patriot as well as a man of God, he did not turn a deaf ear to their appeal. He would not allow personal resentment to override national responsibility.

That he possessed charismatic leadership qualities is clear from the sway he exercised and the loyalty he drew from his band of outlaws. His natural gifts were greatly enhanced by a special enduement of the Spirit, for "the Spirit of the Lord came upon Jephthah" (Judges 11:29). By reason of his anointing, he "enters the list of the charismatic leaders."[2] His was a spiritual authority imparted as the result of a divine commission. Samuel tells us that "the Lord sent . . . Jephthah" as the deliverer of the nation (1 Samuel 12:11).

From the content and tone of the conciliatory message he sent to the Ammonites, we see that Jephthah was familiar with both the Mosaic law and the history of the nation. His roving and irregular life had not robbed him of his genuine piety and fear of God. It is significant that his first action on being elevated to the position of supreme judge was to spread the whole situation before the Lord, perhaps at the tabernacle. "The people made him head and chief over them; and *Jephthah spoke all his words before the Lord at Mizpah*" (Judges 11:11; italics added). His spiritual sensitivity is seen in his seeking divine approval and guidance for the task ahead.

A Skillful Negotiator

The manner in which Jephthah conducted negotiations with the Ammonites, and with the men of Ephraim, in an endeavor to avoid war, shows him to have been a wise man who appreciated the value of a diplomatic approach, and one who would not rush headlong into war. His first judicial act was to send a pacific and courteous message to his aggressive enemies. He was careful to make it clear that any initiative in the hostilities did not come from him and that he was not seeking confrontation.

To the king of Ammon, who pressed the baseless charge that the people of Israel had misappropriated his land

2. F. F. Bruce, "Judges," in *The New Bible Commentary,* D. Guthrie et al., 3d ed. rev. (Grand Rapids: Eerdmans, 1970), p. 268.

when they came up from Egypt, Jephthah gave a calm and clearly-reasoned answer from history. The people of Israel had not misappropriated the lands of Moab and Ammon (Judges 11:15); rather, Jehovah had given the lands to Israel, which held the lands by right of conquest (Judges 11:21). If their god, Chemosh, had given the land to them, should they not have taken possession of it? Balak, king of Moab, had never disputed Israel's claim (Judges 11:24-25). So Israel was guiltless, and Israel's foes were in the wrong in threatening war—they had no cause for offense.

In his negotiations with the irascible Ephraimites, Jephthah displayed a similar conciliatory spirit (Judges 12:1-3). He refuted their angry allegation that they had been ignored. The fact was that he had appealed to them and they had not responded. It appears, however, that Jephthah's subsequent action was unduly harsh.

Although he showed moderation in dealing with others, he would not be imposed on. When the Gileadites made their appeal to him to lead them, his native shrewdness and his past experience with them led him to be cautious in his response. He would not assume the onerous responsibility of leadership until he had it in black and white that they granted him absolute leadership (Judges 11:9-11). He displayed the same shrewdness in the method he adopted to check the nationality of the rebellious Ephraimites (Judges 12:5-6).

A Tragic Vow

Under Jephthah's inspiring leadership, Israel thoroughly vanquished the Ammonites, capturing twenty cities in the process. But before going into battle, he made a vow to the Lord that was to turn his triumph into tragedy. He vowed that in the event of his being victorious, "whatever comes out of the doors of my house to meet me when I return in peace from the sons of Ammon, it shall be the LORD's, and I will offer it up as a burnt offering" (Judges 11:30-31).

Apparently his wife had died, leaving him with an only

child, a daughter. His distress can be imagined when, on his victorious return, his beloved daughter rushed out of the house to greet him.

"Alas, my daughter!" he cried, tearing his clothes in his anguish; "I have given my word to the LORD, and I cannot take it back" (Judges 11:35). It is recorded that at the end of two months, her father "did to her according to the vow which he had made" (Judges 11:39).

The crucial question, which has been endlessly debated over the years, is What exactly did Jephthah do to his daughter in fulfilling his vow? Did he offer her as a burnt offering, or did he devote her to perpetual virginity and the service of the sanctuary? Considerable scholarly authority is ranged on both sides of the question, and it may not be possible to arrive at a categorical answer. Perhaps the most we can do is to adopt the view which seems most in keeping with the revealed character of God.

Was Jephthah's Daughter Sacrificed?

Roman history records a similar vow made by Idomeneus, king of Crete, who on his way home from the Trojan War was overtaken by a terrible storm. In his fear, he vowed that if his life was spared he would sacrifice to the gods whatever should first meet him on his return home. To his dismay, it was his son who first met him.

Porphyry wrote, "The Phoenicians in all great emergencies of war or famine or drought, used to designate by vote one of their nearest and dearest as a sacrifice to Saturn."[3] So in those primitive days, the idea of human sacrifice was well known. But in this case the question arises: Would this be the likely action of a genuine worshiper of Jehovah, a worshiper who displayed familiarity with the Mosaic law, which forbids human sacrifice (Leviticus 18:21)? Would he be likely to vow to do what God had expressly forbidden?

If he did indeed offer his daughter up in sacrifice, it was

---

3. In Arthur Hervey, "Judges," in *Holy Bible with Commentary* (London: John Murray, 1873), 2:184.

either because he did not know of the divine prohibition or because he flagrantly flouted it. It would not appear to be the action of a man of whom it had just been recorded, "Now the Spirit of the LORD came upon Jephthah" (Judges 11:29).

Is there any acceptable alternative interpretation to that which involves human sacrifice? We think there is. The *New American Standard Bible* (1973 ed.) rendering of Judges 11:31 supports this view. It reads: "Whatever comes out of the doors of my house to meet me, . . . it shall be the Lord's, *or* I will offer it up as a burnt offering" (italics added). If there are two possible interpretations, would it not be more in keeping with the revealed character of God to adopt that which is the more humane?

In further support of this view, the provisions of Leviticus 27:1-8 are advanced. In the case of a difficult vow, this passage permits it to be commuted for a monetary payment assessed by the priest. In Jephthah's case, this would mean that if an animal had come out of the house, it would be offered as a burnt offering. If it were a human being, a monetary offering could be made and the person dedicated to the service of the sanctuary.

The case against Jephthah's daughter being literally immolated is well stated by Professor W. G. Moorehead: "In spite of the strong arguments urged in support of the view that he actually offered his daughter in sacrifice to God, in accordance with his vow, there is enough ground in the somewhat ambiguous narrative to justify a more humane interpretation. It seems more in harmony with the place given Jephthah among the saints, and with her 'bewailing her virginity,' that the father devoted his daughter to a life of celibacy and seclusion."[4]

Elements of Nobility

Whichever view is favored, elements of nobility are seen in both father and daughter. In the father, *integrity* and

---

4. W. G. Moorehead, *Outline Studies in the Old Testament* (1893; reprint ed., Grand Rapids: Zondervan, n.d.), p. 78.

faithfulness are the outstanding qualities. Even though it meant he would be tearing out his own heart and that he would die without posterity—a serious thing to a Hebrew—he would fulfill his vow. Mistaken though he doubtless was in making the vow, once it was made he would not allow even paternal affection to deflect him from fulfilling it. His mistake lay not in refusing to be deterred from fulfilling a vow to God, but in the defective and unworthy view of God that had prompted the vow.

The daughter's reply to her father's agonized cry ranks in nobility with that of another virgin. When Jephthah broke the tragic news to his daughter, she responded: "My father, you have given your word to the Lord; do to me as you have said, since the LORD has avenged you of your enemies, the sons of Ammon" (Judges 11:36). Centuries later, in response to the angelic announcement, Mary, the mother of our Lord, replied: "Behold, the bondslave of the Lord; be it done to me according to your word" (Luke 1:38). Jephthah's daughter's piety, her sense of filial duty, and her patriotism mark her out as one of history's great heroines.

Vows in Contemporary Life

What is the biblical teaching concerning vows for our own times? Vows are mentioned only three times in the New Testament, twice by our Lord and once in connection with Paul (Matthew 5:33-37; 23:16-22; Acts 18:18). Interestingly enough, Christ spoke of vows only to condemn their abuse.

In Paul's case, for some reason he had taken a temporary Nazirite vow. It may have been on deliverance from some great danger. He allowed his hair to grow long during the duration of the vow, but before he embarked for Syria he had his hair cut, a sign that the period of the vow had come to an end. In the record, there is nothing said either in favor of or against taking vows. It is left to the Christian conscience. No one should enter into a vow that it is not in his power to perform.

In the Old Testament, vows were always voluntary and

were never regarded as a religious duty (Deuteronomy 23:22). However, once made, they were to be conscientiously performed. "When you make a vow to God, do not be late in paying it, for He takes no delight in fools. Pay what you vow! It is better that you should not vow than that you should vow and not pay" (Ecclesiastes 5:4-5).

A vow was acceptable not as the purchase price of a desired boon; rather, it was generally an expression of gratitude to God. In the light of the great number of vows that are made in time of distress only to be broken, they should be made not on the spur of the moment, but after serious thought, and with a determination to fulfill them. Not the least important of such vows are those made at the marriage altar, which, as the marriage ceremony wisely enjoins, are not to be entered into lightly or inadvisedly, and when taken, are to be faithfully carried out.

8

Samuel

The Man Who Wore Six Hats

"The LORD was with him and let none of his words fall to the ground" (1 Samuel 3:19, marg.).

There are times in the history of nations when a single man is of more value than a multitude of men. This is because quality is more valuable than quantity, and because individual character is more effective than numerical force. Indeed, national life, good or bad, usually reduces itself to the question of man. . . . And so it was, that Samuel, in his time, . . . was the one great factor of life and righteousness between God and Israel.[1]

(Henry W. Frost)

Few leaders of the Jewish nation filled so many roles, and filled them with such distinction, as Samuel. What shall we call him? Priest, prophet, judge, king-maker, educator, nation-builder? He was all those, and he deserves to rank with Abraham and Moses as a leading architect of the nation's destiny.

When it seemed that a decadent and apostate Israel must be engulfed by its enemies, God raised up Samuel as

1. Henry W. Frost, *Men Who Prayed* (Philadelphia: S.S. Times, 1914), p. 123.

its deliverer. He was the last of the judges, and under God he arrested the national drift, consolidated the kingdom, and gave it both education and orderly government. For many years, this massive yet gentle man controlled the destiny of the nation.

When Samuel came to leadership, the nation was in deep trouble. The permissive society that developed during the period of the judges had brought the nation to its lowest moral and spiritual level. As Charles Kingsley said, there are two kinds of freedom—the false, when a man is free to do what he likes; the true, when a man is free to do what he ought. Under the judges, everyone felt free to do "what was right in his own eyes" (Judges 21:25). Democracy ran riot, with resulting moral chaos. But God did not abandon His people, and the instrument He chose to channel moral and spiritual blessing to His people was a childless woman pouring out her wordless sorrow to God (1 Samuel 1:10-11).

Elkanah and his wife Hannah were both devout and devoted. Their home was at Ramathaim-zophim, in the hill country of Ephraim. Polygamy was still practiced in Israel, and the harmony of Elkanah's home was marred by the condescending taunts of his second wife, who had been blessed with some children. Peninnah regarded her children as an evidence of God's special favor, and she regarded Hannah's barrenness as a mark of His disapproval. She made Hannah's life miserable with her taunts and arrogance. Hannah's only refuge was in prayer. Her appeal to God, asking for a son whom she promised to give back to Him, was heard by a loving and concerned God.

The Boon of a Praying Mother

When Hannah visited the temple at Shiloh (1 Samuel 1:9) to pour out her heart, she was roughly treated by Eli, the old priest, who mistook the intensity of her supplication for intoxication (1 Samuel 1:12-13). On realizing the cause of her sorrow, Eli sent her away with a blessing and with the assurance that her request had been granted.

God was as specific in His answer as Hannah had been in her prayer, and she named her son Samuel, which means "asked of God." Is it surprising that with this background the child should become one of the world's great intercessors? Abraham Lincoln claimed that all he was or ever hoped to be, he owed to his angel mother.[2] Samuel would doubtless have said the same, for Hannah was among the nobility of the Bible.

Her hymn of thanksgiving for God's gift ranks in beauty with Mary's magnificat and undoubtedly was its inspiration (1 Samuel 2:1-10; Luke 1:46-55). Hannah was true to her costly vow, and in due time she presented her son to God at the temple. For four years she had denied herself the pleasure of the social intercourse and festivities of the annual pilgrimage to Shiloh so that she could devote herself to the care of her son. But there was no repining on her part (1 Samuel 1:21-28).

There are both beauty and pathos in the relationship of the little lad to Eli, the genial but negligent priest. His wayward sons, Hophni and Phinehas, were worthless fellows who despised the privileges of their office. They crudely violated the laws of sacrifice to gratify their undisciplined appetites. God views the sin of such sacrilege and irreverence very seriously (1 Samuel 2:17).

With all his good points, Eli had been a weak father who made only ineffectual efforts to control his sons. Like many another father, his discipline was too little and too late. His crowning failure was that he honored his sons above God (1 Samuel 2:29), and for that he reaped a bitter harvest. What a contrast there is between the sweetness and purity of little Samuel and the debauchery of the sons of Eli. While they were wallowing in their sin, "Samuel was growing in stature and in favor both with the LORD and with men" (1 Samuel 2:26).

The Call of God

In the lives of most men and women who have achieved distinction in the work of the Kingdom, there has been some significant experience in which they have discerned

---

2. In Clarence Edward Macartney, *The Greatest Men of the Bible* (New York: Abingdon-Cokesbury, 1941), p. 148.

the call of God. It came early to Samuel. The story of God's thrice-repeated call and the boy's ready response has delighted children down the centuries. No longer spiritually sensitive, Eli did not at first realize that it was the Lord who was calling Samuel. Then he instructed the lad how to respond if the call came again: "Speak, Lord, for Thy servant is listening" (1 Samuel 3:9).

God may not now speak to us audibly as He did to Samuel, but we can still hear His authoritative voice through His Word. It is when we are ready to obey that we hear it most distinctly.

> O give me Samuel's heart:
>   A lowly heart that waits
> Where in Thy house Thou art,
>   Or watches at Thy gates!
> By day and night, a heart that still
> Moves at the breathing of Thy will.
>
> (James D. Burns)

Confucius once said that the great man is he who does not lose his "child's" heart. The message that came to the lad Samuel filled him with foreboding. How could he convey such a message of doom (1 Samuel 3:11-14) to his kindly old friend? At first he shrank from breaking the news to Eli; but at the old man's insistence, he "told him everything and hid nothing from him" (1 Samuel 3:18). Something of his old nobility shone out in Eli's response: "It is the Lord; let Him do what seems good to Him" (1 Samuel 3:18).

This solemn experience was Samuel's initiation into the prophetic office, for "all Israel . . . knew that Samuel was confirmed as a prophet of the Lord" (1 Samuel 3:20). Josephus tells us that Samuel was only twelve when the Lord appeared to him. There is urgent need in the pulpits of our land for prophets like Samuel who will not fear to declare all the counsel of God, both mercy and judgment, although it may not be popular. There are still times when a lone prophetic voice can exercise a more potent influence than the voice of the multitude.

Samuel the Judge

After Eli's tragic death, the responsibility of judging Israel devolved on Samuel (1 Samuel 7:6). The judges of Israel were not a regular succession of leaders; they were occasional deliverers whom God raised up to lead His people and administer justice in times of acute crisis. In the course of his duties, with Ramah as his center, Samuel conducted an annual circuit to Bethel, Gilgal, and Mizpah, establishing equity and justice in a disordered nation. He filled this office until his death (1 Samuel 7:15).

The defeat of Israel by the Philistines and the loss of the sacred ark of the Lord were a demoralizing blow to the nation (1 Samuel 4:10-11). The prophetic utterance of the wife of Phinehas proved only too true: she had named her son "Ichabod, saying, 'The glory has departed from Israel' " (1 Samuel 4:21). God had left His people to their chosen ways. They had to learn the hard way that they could not trifle with God.

Under Samuel's prayerful and wise leadership a more healthy spiritual climate began to develop. His call to repentance carried with it the assurance of divine help. "If you return to the LORD with all your heart, remove the foreign gods and Ashtaroth from among you" (1 Samuel 7:3). The people repented, and in response to Samuel's intercession, the Lord granted them deliverance (1 Samuel 7:8-12).

One of the sorrows of this great man's life was that his sons brought him no joy. The tragedy he had seen enacted so vividly before his eyes in the case of Eli and his sons was repeated, though to a less degree, in his own, for his sons "did not walk in his ways, but turned aside after dishonest gain and took bribes and perverted justice" (1 Samuel 8:3).

Samuel was not the last father to suffer this experience. Scripture does not reveal with whom the blame for the misdeeds of his sons lay, but the father must bear some measure of responsibility, if not for their actions, at least for their continuance in office. He was in a position of supreme authority and could not be held guiltless. It is all too true that we learn from history that men do not learn from history.

The Pathway of Rejection

It was a bitter blow for the prophet when the elders of the nation refused to ratify his appointment of his sons as judges over Israel. One wonders how such a man could allow parental affection and ambition to put forward such a proposal. It marks him as a man of like passions and failings with ourselves.

The nation rejected his leadership and demanded that he appoint a king. "Now appoint a king for us to judge us like all the nations" was their cry (1 Samuel 8:5). Samuel realized that the nation had reached a point of great crisis, and his sorrow was deepened by the consciousness that his failure with his family had precipitated it. With prophetic insight, he knew that their request was in reality a repudiation of the theocracy—the rule of the nation by God—and that they were demanding a monarchy, so that they would have a government like that of the other nations. God's intention was that Israel should be *unlike* other nations and own allegiance directly and only to Him. They wanted to be *like* the other nations.

No leader enjoys being rejected, and Samuel had been more than usually unselfish and altruistic in his service. The Lord was gentle with him in the hour of his bitterness and pointed out that He was sharing His servant's rejection. "Listen to the voice of the people," the Lord counseled him, "in regard to all that they say to you, for they have not rejected you, but they have rejected Me from being king over them" (1 Samuel 8:7). So that they would enter the arrangement with their eyes wide open, God charged Samuel to warn them of the heavy cost to them if their request were granted (1 Samuel 8:11-18).

The people were tired of having only an invisible Leader, however, and were not to be dissuaded. They wanted someone they could see and manipulate. But how true Samuel's warning proved to be. When Rehoboam became king the people complained, "Your father made our yoke hard; therefore lighten the hard service of your father and his heavy yoke which he put on us." To their dismay he replied, "My father disciplined you with whips, but I will discipline you with scorpions" (1 Kings 12:4, 11).

A Man of Stature

Samuel's stature is revealed in the manner in which he reacted to his rejection. He displayed neither anger nor petulance, but proceeded to do as God had instructed him and appointed a king. So he added to his functions that of king-maker.

Laying aside his personal feelings, he secretly anointed Saul the son of Kish to be king of Israel. The appointment was later ratified by the nation. Saul began his career under propitious circumstances, and from the beginning he had Samuel's fullest support and loyalty, although he was as faithful in rebuke as he was in encouragement.

It would be difficult to conceive a more noble and dignified valedictory than that of Samuel. He reminded the people of his altruism and integrity in the conduct of his office from childhood to old age. He requested a full vindication of his administration in the presence of the king (1 Samuel 12:1-3), challenging anyone to bring any charge against his honesty. The depth of his love and concern for the nation found expression in his closing words, "As for me, far be it from me that I should sin against the LORD by ceasing to pray for you" (1 Samuel 12:23).

As Samuel saw the steady deterioration of Saul's character over the years, he was heartbroken. At length the word of the Lord came to him, " 'I regret that I have made Saul king. . . .' and Samuel was distressed and cried out to the LORD all night" (1 Samuel 15:11). The final break came when Saul's apostasy became fixed. "And Samuel did not see Saul again until the day of his death; for Samuel grieved over Saul" (1 Samuel 15:35).

One of Samuel's distinctive contributions to the life of the nation was in the realm of theological education. We are told that before his own call to the priesthood "word from the LORD was rare in those days, visions were infrequent" (1 Samuel 3:1). But after he was established as a prophet, "the LORD revealed Himself to Samuel at Shiloh by the word of the LORD" (1 Samuel 3:21).

Schools of the Prophets

It was as prophet that Samuel probably made one of his most potent contributions to the spiritual and cultural life of the people. Under his inspiration there sprang up bands of prophets, or schools of the prophets. They appear in 1 Samuel 10:5, when for the first time the organized prophets were heard. We are not given precise information as to the form in which these theological colleges or Bible schools were organized, but under Samuel's wise guidance they exercised a notable function.

After Samuel's death, the schools of the prophets were not mentioned again until the times of Elijah and Elisha, who drew much support from their help and doubtless also gave help in their direction. After the death of Elisha no more is heard of them. They had filled a most important function in preserving the purity of the Lord's message.

A Man of Prayer

No treatment of the prophet would be complete without reference to the place of prayer in his life and ministry. He was born and nurtured in prayer, and his early years were spent in the house of prayer. He was sensitive and responsive to the voice of God. His early response, "Speak, for Thy servant is listening" (1 Samuel 3:10), could be written over his whole life.

"Praying Samuels come from praying Hannahs, . . . [and] praying leaders come from praying homes," wrote Edward M. Bounds.[3] In times of national crisis, Samuel's first resort was to prayer. His message to the threatened nation was "Gather all Israel to Mizpah, and I will pray to the LORD for you" (1 Samuel 7:5). And the people believed in the

3. Edward M. Bounds, *Prayer and Praying Men* (New York: Doran, 1921), p. 82.

efficacy of his intercessions. "Do not cease to cry to the LORD our God for us, that He may save us from the hand of the Philistines" (1 Samuel 15:11). Small wonder that Jeremiah classed him along with Moses as one of the great intercessors (Jeremiah 15:1).

From the frequency with which Samuel's story is linked with his life of prayer, it will be seen that to him prayer was not a mere addendum to his spiritual exercises, but their very lifeblood. The psalmist pays his tribute to the potency of Samuel's prayers: "Moses and Aaron were among His priests, and Samuel was among those who called on His name; they called upon the LORD, and He answered them" (Psalm 99:6).

The Witch of Endor

Samuel's story did not end with his death. He came back from the shades of Sheol and preached to Saul. Without Samuel's support, Saul was in a bad way. When the Philistines attacked again, he was beside himself with fear. Not only had he lost Samuel, he had lost God too. He had to see his old friend Samuel again and obtain his counsel, for no dreams or visions came to guide him now. In his despair, he disregarded God's explicit command and resorted to the witch of Endor for comfort.

The lamentable spectacle of a proud king disguising himself and slinking off at the dead of night to consult a witch marked the nadir of his career. Guaranteeing her immunity from punishment, he asked her to use her incantations to call up Samuel from the dead (1 Samuel 28:3-25). To the consternation of both medium and king, God Himself interrupted the seance by causing not an impersonating spirit, but Samuel himself to appear in person.

The passage is not without its problems of interpretation, but it should be noted that it explicitly states, "Then Samuel said to Saul" (1 Samuel 28:15). This categorical statement of Scripture precludes the possibility that it was an evil spirit impersonating Samuel. It would seem that God had permitted Samuel to appeal to Saul, but only to deliver to him the last terrible message of his rejection. To his dismay he discovered that Samuel was still on God's side.

That this was an actual appearance of Samuel is evidenced by the surprise and terror of the medium at the unexpected result of her necromancy. The exact fulfillment of Samuel's prophecy in the death of Saul made it clear that God had indeed spoken through His prophet. Obviously Samuel did not appear merely at the call of the medium, else why should she be astonished and cry with a loud voice? God does not permit the spirits of His departed children to be at the whim or command of godless mediums on earth.

Was this permitted appearance of Samuel, like our Lord's final appeal to Judas, a last gracious endeavor on God's part to lead Saul back to the path of repentance and confession?

Even after death it could be said of Samuel, as of Abel, that "though he is dead, he still speaks" (Hebrews 11:4).

9

Solomon

The King with the Empty Heart

"I have seen all the works which have been done under the sun, and behold, all is vanity and striving after wind" (Ecclesiastes 1:14).

Here was a king who inherited his father's love and his kingdom, increased its boundaries by his sagacity; made commerce to flourish by extensive voyages of his ships to Ophir and India (I Kings 10:22, 23); a man noted for his literary pursuits and scientific curiosity "from the cedar that is in Lebanon even to the hyssop that springeth out of the wall; who spake also of beasts and birds and creeping things and fishes" (I Kings 4:32). The splendour of his court, the magnificence of his table, his pomp and wealth became proverbial; distinguished men and women came from afar to hear his wisdom and seek his counsel (I Kings 10:1-25); and yet the question he himself raises is that he is an unhappy monarch, a restless soul, and a lonely lover.[1]

(Samuel Marinus Zwemer)

In the sacred books of each of the great theistic faiths—the Hebrew Scriptures, the New Testament, and the Ko-

1. Samuel Marinus Zwemer, *Sons of Adam* (Grand Rapids: Baker, 1951), pp. 123-24.

ran—Solomon is accorded an honored place. The Koran devotes no fewer than six chapters to his wisdom and renown. In three New Testament passages our Lord Himself bore testimony to his wisdom and greatness and glory (Matthew 6:29; 12:42; Luke 11:31).

In many ways his forty-year reign eclipsed those of his two predecessors in both glory and achievement. But his history also shows that the man who above all others had the capacity, facilities, and resources to explore to the full all the pleasures of mind and body the world can offer came at last to the mournful conclusion "All is vanity and striving after wind" (Ecclesiastes 1:14).

> A king dwelt in Jerusalem:
> He was the wisest man on earth.
> He had all riches from his birth,
> And pleasures till he tired of them.
> Then having tested all things, he
> Witnessed that all was vanity.
>
> (Christina Rossetti)

Solomon was David's tenth son, the second by Bathsheba, the former wife of Uriah the Hittite. It was not until he was an old man that David, in order to forestall an attempted coup by his son Adonijah, was compelled to arrange hastily for Solomon to be anointed as king. At the time, Solomon was about fifteen, according to Josephus. As the throne of so young a king would not be secure while his enemies were alive, David instructed Solomon how to treat them after his death. Solomon followed his father's advice, probably too ruthlessly.

A Challenge to the Throne

The first challenge came to Solomon when Adonijah, through Solomon's mother, made the seemingly innocuous request that he should be given Abishag, the wife of David's old age. As David's wife she would be considered an inheritor, and with her would go the rights to the throne. Solomon saw in the request a subtle ruse by which Adonijah again sought to gain his objective, and it could be a move toward rebellion. He had pardoned Adonijah for his previous action, but not this time (1 Kings 2:13-25). Adonijah and the other rebels and rivals to Solomon's throne were liquidated, and Solomon was able to devote his powers to the consolidation of his kingdom.

Although his reign began auspiciously and ultimately reached the highest peak of earthly glory in Israel's history, ominous signs early began to appear. First, he entered on a series of politically advantageous marriages to non-Hebrew women; however, the marriages proved to be spiritually disastrous. His first alliance was with the daughter of the powerful king of Egypt.

It was a diplomatic victory, but it proved to be a step of compromise that led to tragedy. There were reservations in his devotion to Jehovah that finally led to idolatry and apostasy: "Solomon loved the LORD, walking in the statutes of his father David, except he sacrificed and burned incense on the high places" (1 Kings 3:3). The sinister significance of the word "except" will be appreciated when it is realized that those high places were considered sacred to the worship of the Canaanite deities.

A Wise Choice

When Solomon visited the sanctuary at Gibeon to offer sacrifices, the Lord appeared to him in a dream. The Lord's invitation, "Ask what you wish me to give you" (1 Kings 3:5), was a searching test of the young man's motivation and ambitions. What would he ask? We might profitably put the same question to ourselves. What is it we desire supremely of God?

Deeply conscious of his own immaturity and inexperience in matters of state, Solomon humbly put the interests of his people before his own and made this memorable response: "Give Thy servant an understanding heart to judge Thy people to discern between good and evil. For who is able to judge this great people of Thine?" (1 Kings 3:9). Solomon desired above all else to have a genuine and sympathetic involvement in the lives of the people and to rule them wisely.

The Lord's response to his request surpassed anything Solomon had dreamed. Not only was his petition granted, but riches, honor, victory, and long life were thrown in as a bonus. This Old Testament incident anticipated and illustrated the Lord's words in the Sermon on the Mount: "Seek first His kingdom and His righteousness; and all these things shall be added to you" (Matthew 6:33).

It should be noted, however, that it was not for the spiritual wisdom so frequently commended in Scripture that Solomon asked. It was more sagacity and skill in guiding the affairs of his kingdom, rather than insight into divine things, that he desired. Nevertheless, "it was pleasing in the sight of the Lord that Solomon had asked this thing" (1 Kings 3:10).

In his skillful solution to the seemingly insoluble problem presented by the two harlots and the dead baby (1 Kings 3:16-28), he gave early evidence of divinely imparted wisdom, and he greatly enhanced his own prestige. "Solomon's wisdom surpassed the wisdom of all the sons of the east and all the wisdom of Egypt. . . . And his fame was known in all the surrounding nations" (1 Kings 4:30-31).

Prodigious Achievements

From his writings it may be gleaned that he possessed specialized knowledge in botany, zoology, horticulture, architecture, philosophy, and literature. His own literary output is astounding. "He also spoke 3,000 proverbs, and his songs were 1,005" (1 Kings 4:32).

A proverb has been defined as "the wit of one embodying the wisdom of many." We need not assume that all the proverbs Solomon collated were orginal, but they were the product of his wit and wisdom. It would seem that he wrote the Song of Songs in his early years, collated the book of Proverbs in middle life, and wrote the book of Ecclesiastes in old age. Each book reflects his outlook on life at the relevant period.

In the material realm, Solomon's achievements were equally prodigious. With his wide-sweeping fleets and widespread trade treaties, he brought great commercial prosperity to the nation. By astute diplomacy he enlarged the boundaries of his kingdom until under his rule Israel attained its great geographical extent. Through the connections of his seven hundred wives many advantageous alliances were forged. Some of those wives were daughters of tributary chiefs, given as hostages for their fathers' good behavior.

Although his reign was an era of peace, Solomon did not neglect the defense of his country. At his disposal as commander-in-chief were 1,400 chariots and 12,000 horsemen (2 Chronicles 1:14). He had 4,000 stalls for horses and chariots (2 Chronicles 9:25), and he conducted a lucrative trade in horses and chariots with the Hittites and Egyptians.

The wealth flowing into his treasuries from commerce, tribute, and taxation was astronomical. "Now the weight of gold which came in to Solomon in one year was 666 talents of gold, besides that from the traders and the wares of the merchants and all the kings of the Arabs and the governors of the country. . . . All King Solomon's drinking vessels were of gold. . . . None was of silver; it was not considered valuable in the days of Solomon" (1 Kings 10:14-15, 21). The magnificence of his court and the sumptuousness of his table were proverbial.

The Missing Element

But amid all the glory and majesty of Solomon's reign, the spiritual element was notably absent. The keen insight and theological awareness so evident in his prayer at the opening of the Temple showed that he had a great capacity for the spiritual, but in his pursuit of pleasure he allowed the spiritual side of his nature to atrophy.

In building the Temple and his own palace, Solomon found abundant scope for his architectural brilliance, and his great wealth enabled him to achieve anything he fancied. His slipping scale of values, however, is hinted at in the fact that he devoted seven years to building God's house and thirteen years to his own. The Temple he built was notable not so much for its size as for its lavish and aesthetic beauty. Though patterned after the tabernacle, it was much more ornate and complex.

The zenith of Solomon's career was reached in his prayer at the dedication of the Temple (1 Kings 8:22-53). Not without reason it has been adjudged one of the grandest devotional utterances to be found in pre-Christian literature. In the prayer itself, which breathes a sense of the divine majesty, he appealed to God to hear the prayers of His people.

His requests were specific: for continuing divine blessing and protection (vv. 25-30), for judgment of the wicked and vindication of the righteous (vv. 31-32), for deliverance when sin has been repented of and confessed (vv. 33-40), for help for the pious stranger (vv. 41-43), for victory in battle (vv. 44-45), and for forgiveness for national sins (vv. 46-53).

The falling of fire from heaven marked God's acceptance of the king's prayer. "When Solomon had finished praying, fire came down from heaven and consumed the burnt offering and the sacrifices; and the glory of the LORD filled the house" (2 Chronicles 7:1). So overwhelming was the manifestation of the divine glory that the priests could not enter the Temple to discharge their duties. The reaction of the people was spontaneous. But the high resolve and emotional response evoked by the appearing of the Shekinah glory proved transient.

The account of the visit of the queen of Sheba to King Solomon's court has become world famous. It is generally thought that she was the ruler of the Sabeans, who lived in Araba Felix, which is known today as the Yemen. In keeping with traditional royal custom, the queen was anxious to discover whether there was basis in fact for the fabulous reports of the king's wisdom. After she had put him through his hoops, had seen the magnificence of his palace with its ivory throne, the luxury of his table, and the bearing of his courtiers, she was breathless.

"It was a true report which I heard in my own land about your words and your wisdom," she gasped. "Nevertheless I did not believe the reports, until I came and my eyes had seen it. And behold, the half was not told me. You exceed

in wisdom and prosperity the report which I heard"
(1 Kings 10:6-7).

The Other Side of the Coin

But now for the other side of the coin. The tragedy of
Solomon's meteoric career was that in spite of his honored
ancestry, vast wisdom, brilliant gifts, staggering wealth,
and outwardly successful reign, his life was a steady de-
scent into disillusionment and apostasy.

In a rather severe assessment of Solomon's character
and achievements, Dr. W. Graham Scroggie asserts that
there are only four things known to his credit—his voice
of wisdom, his prayer of dedication, his benediction after
the dedication, and Psalm 72. On the adverse side are his
questionable severity in his executions, his unrestrained
polygamy, his multiplication of horses and chariots, his
use of slave labor, his condoning of idol worship, his vast
accumulation of wealth, his luxurious despotism, his foreign alliances, and his flagrant irreligion.[2] Whether or not
we fully endorse these strictures, there is sufficient sub-
stance in them to reveal the emptiness of a life in which
God is given a diminishing place.

During Solomon's reign, the court was supreme and the
priesthood secondary. No prophets arose. Unlike his predecessors Saul and David, Solomon experienced no prophetic afflatus. The fact that the word of the Lord came to
him only once revealed the poverty of his reign despite its
material splendor. With advancing years, he grew less responsive to the divine.

A number of factors contributed to his steady decline. He
disobeyed the wise Mosaic regulations concerning Israel's
king. They were clear. "He shall not multiply horses for
himself. . . . Neither shall he multiply wives for himself; . . .
nor shall he greatly increase silver and gold for himself"
(Deuteronomy 17:16-17). He did all those things to a flagrant degree.

---

2. W. Graham Scroggie, *The Unfolding Drama of Redemption*, 3 vols.
(Old Tappan, N.J.: Revell, 1953), 1:270-71.

Instead of relying on Jehovah for protection from his foes, Solomon put his confidence in chariots and horses. His blatant polygamy inevitably led him into blatant idolatry and weaned his heart away from the God of Israel. It was written of good King Hezekiah, "He clave to the Lord" (2 Kings 18:6, KJV). Of Solomon it is recorded, "Solomon loved many . . . women. . . . Solomon clave unto these in love" (1 Kings 11:1-2, KJV). He sacrificed the favor of God for sensual delight, and it turned to ashes in his mouth. His syncretism in religion became a potent source of weakness to the nation.

His vast wealth was accumulated only at the price of the crippling taxation of his subjects. The erection of prestigious buildings was achieved only at the cost of impressing slave labor on a large scale. The people admired his brilliance and basked in the reflected glory of his reign, but they writhed under the crushing burdens he placed on them. He never won their affection as his father, David, had done.

The organization of Solomon's kingdom on a regional basis was a brilliant success, but the individual was lost in the vast and soulless machine. In the present day of automation and passion for bigness and statistics in the work of the church, we too are apt to lose sight of the individual.

Instead of basing his reign securely on loyalty to God, as his father had done, Solomon resorted to the political ploy of marriage alliances with foreign powers. Far from stabilizing his kingdom, it proved his undoing. "Now the LORD was angry with Solomon because his heart was turned away from the LORD, the God of Israel, who had appeared to him twice. . . . Then the LORD raised up an adversary to Solomon. . . . God also raised up another adversary to him. . . . Then Jeroboam . . . rebelled against the king" (1 Kings 11:9, 14, 23, 26). The era of peace had run out.

The Acid Test

The true test of the quality of a man's work may be seen in what happens to it after his departure. Solomon left little behind him that was lasting. The kingdom was divided. Even his glorious Temple was later destroyed. "So Israel has been in rebellion against the house of David to this day" (2 Chronicles 10:19) is the dismal epitaph.

Did Solomon show repentance before he died? There is no direct evidence that he did, but some have seen in his book of Ecclesiastes not only an autobiographical confession of the failure of a life lived for things "under the sun," but also a belated and reluctant repentance. It is without doubt the saddest book in the Old Testament, revealing as it does the empty and lonely heart of the old king.

> I said of laughter, it is vain:
> Of mirth I said, What profits it?
> Therefore I found a book and writ
> Therein how ease and also pain,
> How health and sickness, every one
> Is vanity beneath the sun.
>
> (Christina Rossetti)

Was the book a late endeavor to atone somewhat for his own failure by warning others through the medium of recounting his own disillusionment? We can hope that it was so.

In espousing this charitable view, Dr. Samuel Marinus Zwemer wrote, "When, in reading the Bible, we step out of the closet of David into the palace-porch of Solomon we must judge both of these men by their best and not by their worst. It was Solomon who learned at last what he wrote: 'Trust in the Lord with all thine heart and lean not unto thine own understanding. . . . The path of the just is as the shining light that shineth more and more unto the perfect day' (Proverbs 3:5; 4:18)."[3]

10

Jonah

A Preacher Discouraged by Success

"You had compassion on the plant. . . . And should I not have compassion on Nineveh?" (Jonah 4:10-11).

Unbelievers may laugh as much as they please at one of the incidents related in this book, but the book itself condemns them. Here it stands in the majesty of its moral teaching, part of the Jewish Scriptures, quoted by the prophet Joel, referred to by Josephus and in the Apocrypha, and most solemnly endorsed by our blessed Saviour. And while it is easy to make light of the incident of Jonah and the whale, it is impossible to find any reasonable explanation of how the book came to be written if the incidents recorded never took place.[1]

(F. S. Webster)

"No other book in the Bible has been so greatly maligned, so persistently undervalued, so commonly rejected as the book of Jonah."[2] So wrote Dr. R. J. G. McKnight. As with the story of Noah and the ark, the main objection to the book of Jonah's validity as a genuine piece of history is

1. F. S. Webster, "Is the Book of Jonah Allegory or History?" *The Life of Faith*, March 15, 1916, p. 288.
2. R. J. G. McKnight, "The Book of Jonah," *Bible League Quarterly*, July 1928, p. 153.

that it is contrary to science and violates natural law. In other words, it is the supernatural element that is unacceptable.

But if we postulate God, and as Christians we do, miracles are not only possible, but credible. If we try to rid Christianity of its miraculous element, we destroy it. Did not Jesus appeal to His miracles as evidence of His deity? And His resurrection was the greatest miracle of all. There is a miracle involved in this story, but the miracle is far from being its most important feature.

Those who find it difficult to accept the book as history regard it in various ways. Some consider that it is intended to be a parable or allegory. Some treat it as poetry, and others as myth or legend. Yet others view it as a funny story, told with the purpose of pouring ridicule on the bigotry and exclusiveness of the Jewish nation. The prophet himself has become a synonym for the person who brings bad luck. But none of those views plays fair with either the book or its author.

Evidence of Historicity

There is a strong line of evidence to support the view that Jonah was as much a historical figure as his two contemporaries, Hosea and Amos, or as Joel, who quotes from the book. Jonah had already had a successful career as a prophet in the reign of Jeroboam II (see 2 Kings 14:23-27). Jonah's father, Amittai, is named here as well as in Jonah 1:1, and his home is said to be Gath-hepher, the modern Meshed. Nineveh, the city to which he was sent, was one of the oldest capitals of the world. Judged by any standard, the record gives the impression of a genuine historical personage.

For one who accepts the authority of Christ and of the Scriptures, the verdict of our Lord is the end of all argument. If language means anything, He confirmed the historicity of both the man and his book. Jesus' testimony is precise and specific: "An evil and adulterous generation craves for a sign; and yet no sign shall be given to it but the sign of Jonah the prophet; for just as JONAH WAS THREE

DAYS AND THREE NIGHTS IN THE BELLY OF THE SEA MONSTER, so shall the Son of Man be three days and three nights in the heart of the earth. The men of Nineveh shall stand up with this generation at the judgment, and shall condemn it because they repented at the preaching of Jonah; and behold, something greater than Jonah is here. The Queen of the South shall rise up with this generation at the judgment and shall condemn it, because she came from the ends of the earth to hear the wisdom of Solomon; and behold, something greater than Solomon is here" (Matthew 12:39-42).

Jesus here referred to Jonah as a real prophet in the same breath as He spoke of the monarchs known to history, Solomon and the queen of Sheba. The men of Nineveh were real men who will stand in the Judgment. Jonah preached at Nineveh, and Jesus confirmed the successful issue of his ministry. He endorsed the incident of the sea monster.

In the light of such clear assertions, is it conceivable that Jesus would refer to a story He knew to be pure myth as a fact of history? Were He to have done so, He would have been less than straightforward.

Having said that, however, it should be recognized that although the story of Jonah is historically attested, it is at the same time an important treatment of one of the greatest problems of our own generation—narrow racialism. We must see that the central message and purpose of the book is not lost in profitless controversy.

A Frank Confession

This little piece of autobiography rivals Augustine's *Confessions* in the frankness of its self-revelation. Jonah does not spare himself, and he tones down nothing. He exposes his guilt, his insularity, his cowardice, and his lack of love for races other than his own.

From these confessions we can form a reasonably accurate picture of the man. He was a son of the manse, for his father too was a prophet, and he was probably the first of the writing prophets. He appears to have been of a fickle and mercurial temperament, his actions governed more by mood and impulse than by calm judgment. But he partook of the narrowest intolerance and exclusiveness of the nation to which he belonged. He loved his people with a fierce love and hated their enemies with an equally fierce hatred. Was it not this ardent patriotism that in large measure lay at the root of his defection?

Jonah commenced his book with the bald statement of the unwelcome call from God that came to him: "Arise, go to Nineveh the great city, and cry against it, for their wickedness has come up before Me" (Jonah 1:2). We shall not be able to sense Jonah's feelings when this dangerous commission came to him unless we remember that the Assyrians were the most ruthless race on earth. They delighted in violence and brutality. The prophet's reluctance to become the messenger of divine judgment to a city such as this becomes understandable. Let the reader put himself in Jonah's shoes and imagine the tumult of emotions the situation would evoke. He will then have more sympathy for the reluctant prophet when he reads, "but Jonah rose up to flee" (Jonah 1:3).

One can sense the internal struggle. How futile to think that one lone man could exercise any significant influence on the most powerful city on earth! And who would listen to him in any case? Obeying God would be putting one's head right in the lion's mouth.

Strange Motivation

Jonah's loyalty to God was swamped by the inducements to disobey—fear of the Assyrians, ingrained bigotry that wished to monopolize God for his own nation, hatred of the enemy, and the futility of the task. All these motives were doubtless present, but there was one that outweighed them all. Strikingly enough that motive was the love and mercy and forbearance of God.

Why should those wonderful qualities of the divine nature move Jonah to disobey God? Because Jonah knew Him! Behind his recalcitrance lay the certain knowledge that if his mission were successful and Nineveh repented,

God would relent and be merciful to its people. Jonah hated them, and would sooner see them overwhelmed with judgment than pardoned by God.

This all comes out in Jonah's petulant appeal to God to take his life. "Please Lord, was not this what I said while I was still in my own country? Therefore, in order to forestall this I fled to Tarshish, for I knew that Thou art a gracious and compassionate God, slow to anger and abundant in lovingkindness, and *one who relents concerning calamity*" (Jonah 4:2, italics added).

As Jonah faced the issues, the conflict of conscience was so acute that he broke and fled to Joppa. Providentially a ship was ready to sail for Tarshish—the Greek port of Tartessos, Spain. In those days, a ship of Tarshish was a synonym for a first-class vessel. So Jonah paid first-class "to go . . . from the presence of the Lord" (Jonah 1:3). When we try to fly from duty, we shall usually discover that there is a boat just ready to sail, but the fare will be steep!

The prophet wished to put the greatest possible distance between himself and his loathsome task. Nineveh was five hundred miles to the east, and Tarshish two thousand miles to the west. How could he face returning home if he obeyed God and delivered the warning to Nineveh, and then God relented and pardoned the Ninevites? His impeccable record as a prophet would be gone and his reputation shattered. Better to flee than to be discredited!

Jonah must have forgotten the psalm that he had committed to memory as a boy: "Where can I go from Thy Spirit? Or where can I flee from Thy presence? If I ascend to heaven, Thou art there; if I make my bed in Sheol, behold, Thou art there" (Psalm 139:7-8).

The Hound of Heaven

Suddenly the fearsome storm that the Lord had appointed (arranged) broke. Then followed in quick succession the danger of imminent shipwreck, the jettisoning of cargo, the rousing of the sleeping prophet, the challenge to him to call on his God—all told in the vivid words of the main actor. When lots were cast to determine with whom the blame for the calamity lay, it fell, of course, on Jonah.

Throughout the crisis, latent elements of nobility in Jonah's character shone out. No trace of cowardice surfaced. He conducted himself with dignified calm. He recognized that "The Hound of Heaven," to use Francis Thompson's graphic phrase, had at last overtaken him. He well knew the reason behind the storm, and in it he discerned the chastening hand of God, as some of us have done under similar circumstances.

He witnessed faithfully and fearlessly to the pagan crew, affirming his faith in the Lord God who made and controlled the sea's raging. "Pick me up and throw me into the sea," he commanded them. "Then the sea will become calm for you, for I know that on account of me this great storm has come upon you" (Jonah 1:12). They reluctantly obeyed, "and the sea stopped its raging. . . . And the Lord appointed a great fish to swallow Jonah, and Jonah was in the stomach of the fish three days and three nights" (Jonah 1:15-17).

Superficial Misconceptions

It is at this point that ridicule and incredulity are poured upon the story, but there are valid reasons for accepting it as history. The issue has been clouded by superficial misconceptions. Actually, Jonah's experience with the sea monster is only an incidental feature—it is not the central feature of the story. But it is usually so blown up that it conceals the main lesson and purpose of the book. Note some of the factors that are involved.

1. If it be objected that a whale could not swallow a man, or that even if it could, he would not survive the experience, the simple answer is that neither Jonah nor our Lord says that it was a whale. The Hebrew word used is *dag*, which occurs fourteen times in the Old Testament. It always means "a huge fish, a monster of the deep," and it is thus of wider meaning than *whale*. The Hebrew word for whale is *tannin*. The Greek word used by our Lord is *ketos*, which means "sea monster." The whale is not a fish, but a warm-blooded mammal that suckles its young. So

Scripture does not claim that it was a whale that swallowed Jonah.

2. A huge species of shark has been found in the South Seas—with the unmutilated body of a horse in its belly. So the swallowing of a man by such a creature would involve no miracle.[3]

3. In any case, is God more limited than His creatures? God is not the slave of nature, but its Master. If we can suspend or vary the laws of nature by the introduction of a higher law, should God be denied the same power? The natural law is that iron sinks, yet we can interpose a higher law and cause twenty thousand tons of iron to float or a jumbo jet to fly in the air. The Maker of natural law is not the prisoner of His own creation.

4. If it be objected that a man could not remain alive for three days in the belly of the monster, we ask, Where does it say in the record that Jonah stayed alive there? Indeed, on the contrary, our Lord's testimony would imply that he did not stay alive, but experienced resuscitation. If this is so, there is no need to prove that he *could* have stayed alive.

Carefully note the exact words of our Lord's declaration: "*Just as* Jonah was three days and three nights in the belly of the sea monster, *so* shall the Son of Man be three days and three nights in the heart of the earth" (Matt. 12, 40, italics added). Note the "just as, ... so," implying exact equality. In these words, He constitutes Jonah as a type, of which He was the Antitype.

Did Jonah Die?

Dr. Henry W. Frost makes a strong case for Jonah's death while in the sea monster's stomach. On the cross, Christ's body died and was later laid in the tomb. But His spirit did not remain in His body; it went to Sheol, the home of the righteous (Acts 2:25-27). In the miracle of the resurrection, Jesus' spirit returned to the dead body, and in that resurrection body Jesus ascended into heaven. So

3. Ibid., p. 157.

for three days His body was dead in the tomb and His spirit alive in Sheol.[4]

And what of Jonah? Was his experience parallel? If the type is to fit the Antitype, and Jesus said it does, then Jonah's body must have died while his spirit remained alive and conscious, for he cried to the Lord, and was heard (Jonah 2:2). Even in respect to Sheol, the parallel between Jonah and Christ holds good, for did not Jonah say, "I cried for help from the depth of Sheol; Thou didst hear my voice" (Jonah 2:2)? This surely proves that Jonah's body had died, for not bodies but spirits go to Sheol.

Thus it was during the three days and three nights: Jonah's body was dead in the fish, and his spirit was alive in Sheol. At the end of three days, as with the Lord, the spirit returned to the dead body, and the fish deposited the resuscitated Jonah on dry land (Jonah 2:10). If this is the correct interpretation, and it appears to be so, Jonah's experience was not only a type of Christ's resurrection, but a resurrection experience for Jonah himself.

A Unique National Revival

The divine chastening achieved its purpose in the delinquent prophet. When "the word of the LORD came to Jonah the second time" (Jonah 3:1), there was no hesitation, only obedient alacrity. "Jonah arose and went" (Jonah 3:3). Thank God for the second chance, but always remember that the message will be the same as it was the first time!

Picture the lone prophet tramping the long streets of the great city, crying his single message of doom: "Yet forty days and Nineveh will be overthrown" (Jonah 3:4). The power of the Spirit rested on God's now obedient servant, and the result was the most complete national repentance known to Scripture. Not only man, but also beasts displayed the outward signs of repentance, and included were the greatest as well as the least (Jonah 3:5-8).

The king of Nineveh issued a remarkable proclamation:

4. Henry W. Frost, "The Case of Jonah," *The Bible Today* 27, no. 5 (May-June 1933): 147.

"Let men call on God earnestly that each may turn from his wicked way and from the violence which is in his hands. Who knows, God may turn and relent, and withdraw His burning anger so that we shall not perish" (Jonah 3:8-9). And God did just that!

But that was not at all to Jonah's liking. "It greatly displeased Jonah, and he became angry" (Jonah 4:1), so angry that he asked God to take away his life. Instead of leaping for joy at the successful issue of his mission and the display of God's mercy, he went away and sulked. Instead of elating him, his success sank him in the deeps of despondency.

There was a *physiological* contribution to that reaction. Jonah was emotionally and physically drained after his exacting assignment, and apparently he was suffering from sunstroke, for the record runs, "the sun beat down on Jonah's head so that he became faint" (Jonah 4:8). There was also a *selfish* reason—he was engulfed in self-pity, as many of his successors have been! He resented the grace and forbearance of God that had shattered his reputation as a prophet whose word came true. He prophesied judgment, and God exercised mercy. Better to die and have done with it.

There was also a *spiritual* reason for his anger. He was offended in God; God had changed His mind and let him down. How could he ever be sure of his message again? He was a failure, and he might as well end it all. Has the reader ever been tempted to feel that the Lord has let him down and that he will never be able to be sure of His guidance again? That is the reaction of spiritual immaturity. To the mature Christian, it is axiomatic that God *never* lets His children down. Mature Job did not understand God's dealing, but he knew God well enough to say, "Though He slay me, I will hope in Him" (Job 13:15). It is for us to go and do likewise.

Does God Repent?

The preceding paragraph raises a problem: Does God repent? Does He change His mind? The King James Version of Jonah 3:10 has it "God repented of the evil, that he had said that he would do unto them." The *New American Standard* rendering is much to be preferred: "God relented concerning the calamity which He had declared He would bring upon them."

Some interpret this verse to mean that God is fickle and changeable. But it should be remembered that God's threats are conditional: "At one moment I might speak concerning a nation or concerning a kingdom to uproot, to pull down, or to destroy it, *if that nation against which I have spoken turns from its evil, I will relent* concerning the calamity I planned to bring on it" (Jeremiah 18:7-8, italics added).

That is exactly what happened in the case of Nineveh. It was a wicked, violent, and blasphemous nation that God threatened to destroy. But it was a greatly humbled and repentant nation that God pardoned. It is true that "God is not a man, that He should lie, nor a son of man, that He should repent" (Numbers 23:19), but He reserves the right to show mercy to the penitent. While His essential character never changes, He varies His attitude toward men as they alter their attitude toward Him.

Jonah's reaction to God's mercy to the people he hated reveals at once the universal heart of man and the tender love and patience of God. Jonah resigned his commission as a prophet and made outside the city a shelter for himself where he could sit and observe what happened to the city. In his intolerant heart, he cherished the hope that even yet some disaster would overtake it. While he sulked and nursed his resentment against God, he was callously indifferent to the woes of the million people before his eyes.

An Unfinished Symphony

How could this racial prejudice and lack of spiritual concern in His prophet be overcome? God adopted a method adapted to the case. He provided a fast-growing plant—usually thought to be the castor-oil plant—to shelter Jonah from the burning heat of the sun, "and Jonah was extremely happy about the plant" (Jonah 4:6).

But Jonah had to master thoroughly the lesson that is the whole point of the book. So God caused a worm to attack the plant, which withered as rapidly as it had grown. The terrible dust-laden sirocco with its searing heat completed the tragic situation. Jonah was utterly desolated, and he "begged with all his soul to die" (Jonah 4:8). Death was more attractive than life without the sheltering vine.

Then came the still small voice with its gentle but unanswerable logic: "You had compassion on the plant for which you did not work, and which you did not cause to grow, which came up overnight and perished overnight. And *should I not have compassion on Nineveh*, the great city in which there are more than 120,000 persons who do not know the difference between their right and left hand?" (Jonah 4:10-11, italics added). Is not a human soul worth more than a plant?

The book ends so abruptly that it has been termed an unfinished symphony. Unfinished, perhaps so far as Jonah's reactions to the gentle rebuke are concerned, but the silences of Scripture are often remarkably vocal. Is the fact that he wrote the story so honestly an indication that he did learn the lesson? We must hope so.

But the symphony is not unfinished in its wonderful revelation of the heart of God—gracious, compassionate, slow to anger, abundant in loving-kindness. The very abruptness of the ending makes the lesson more vivid.

Although the Jewish nation retained Jonah's prophecy in its Scriptures, it failed to learn the lesson of the book. Even after the Pentecostal effusion and the consequent persecution and dispersion, they preached "to no one except to Jews alone" (Acts 11:19). It was not until a few bold spirits burst through the barriers that some "began speaking to the Greeks also" (Acts 11:20).

Have we learned the lesson? Are we guiltless of lack of concern for the other races and nations of the world? Have we built our shelters of material things in which we sit comfortably watching the world go to the devil? Do we become petulant when God sends a worm to wither our gourd?

Jonah thought his nation was the only land of God;
Jonah held for other lands a stern, prophetic rod,
Would not carry blessings from his own, his native sod:
Jonah knew that God was his.
Called to go to Nineveh, Jonah turned to Spain;
Sought to flee the love of God upon the western main;
Sought to flee God's purposes of pardon, but in vain:
Jonah knew that he was God's.
Once again the word of God that bade the prophet go,
Once again the voice of God announcing bitter woe,
Once again God's mercy which he knew would overflow:
Jonah knew better than God.
Now in mighty Nineveh the prophet's voice is heard:
"Forty days—forty days," a dread, prophetic word;
Souls were moved by mystery, hearts with horror stirred:
Jonah hoped that Nineveh was doomed.
Then the thing happened that Jonah knew would fall,
Nineveh repented at his prophetic call,
God in mercy pardoned after all—after all,
Just as Jonah knew He would.
Jonah on a hilltop, waiting there in gloom;
Jonah moved by pity for a vine's swift doom;
Pity for the vine, but a nation for the tomb:
Did Jonah know at last the love of God?[5]

(Amos R. Wells)

5. Slightly altered from Amos R. Wells, "What Jonah Knew," *S. S. Times* 71, no. 45 (November 9, 1929): 630.

11

Uzziah

The Man Who Was Too Strong

"He was marvelously helped until he was strong. But when he became strong, his heart was so proud that he acted corruptly" (2 Chronicles 26:15-16).

The reign of Uzziah was, to all appearance, extremely prosperous; but his personal character deteriorated, as though it could not bear an unbroken succession of prosperity. Proofs of his genius for empire are furnished by his successful wars. . . . In all these, "he was marvelously helped." How many can bear the same glad witness concerning God's dealings with them! The best preventive of pride is to recognize all blessing as coming from the marvelous help of God.[1]

(F. B. Meyer)

We are all familiar with those days when the sun rises in its ruddy glory and promises warmth and beauty. About midday clouds appear from nowhere and obscure the sun. The temperature drops. Lightning flashes and thunder rolls. The heavens open, and the day that early held such promise closes cold and dark and dismal. Such was the life of the subject of our study.

1. F. B. Meyer, *Through the Bible, Day by Day,* 7 vols. (Philadelphia: Am. S.S. Union, 1914-18), 2:223.

Uzziah, also known as Azariah (1 Chronicles 3:12), was the eleventh king of Judah. Behind him was the inspiration of the memory of a good father, who "did right in the sight of the LORD." But there was a significant qualification about this eulogy—"yet not with a whole heart" (2 Chronicles 25:2). He was hampered by a divided loyalty.

His mother, Jechiliah, was a godly woman who influenced him toward his father's God. He began his reign in a blaze of glory when only sixteen years of age. It was soon evident that he possessed natural gifts that fitted him for his high office, and God blessed and enhanced them so long as he retained his dependence on Him. In his earlier years he displayed true humility and was brilliant, diligent, and enterprising.

The factor that made his long reign of fifty-two years so auspicious, however, was not his gifts or prowess, but that "he did right in the sight of the LORD" (2 Chronicles 26:4). He leaned heavily on his spiritual adviser, Zechariah, who encouraged the young and inexperienced king to seek the Lord for wisdom and guidance in ruling his kingdom. (This prophet was not the author of the prophecy of Zechariah.) He was without doubt the paramount influence in the king's life at that stage. Many have good reason to thank God for the wise counsel and encouragement of a mature Christian in the early and formative years of their Christian lives.

As with his father, there was a qualification in Uzziah's following God. "As long as Zechariah, his religious adviser was living, he served the LORD faithfully, and God blessed him" (2 Chronicles 26:5, TEV*). After Zechariah's stabilizing influence was withdrawn, the deterioration that led to Uzziah's downfall set in.

Unbroken Success and Prosperity

God's blessing on the young king included the gift of unusual wisdom in guiding the destiny of his realm. He had come to the throne at a critical time, but "as long as he

Good News Bible: The Bible in Today's English Version.

sought the LORD, God prospered him" (2 Chronicles 26:5).
During his long reign he greatly enhanced the power and
prestige of the nation and achieved notable military successes. To the west, he subdued the Philistines (2 Chronicles 26:6); to the south, he subdued the Arabians
(2 Chronicles 26:7); to the east, he made the Ammonites
tributary without fighting a battle (2 Chronicles 26:8). All
during Uzziah's reign, Judah lived at peace with the
Northern Kingdom of Israel. He fortified Jerusalem by
building towers at strategic points (2 Chronicles 26:9).
From the military and political angle, his reign rivaled or
even excelled that of his ancestor Solomon.

While waging war on his enemies, Uzziah did not make
the mistake of neglecting his home front; rather, he devoted his considerable organizing ability to developing the
natural resources of the country. Large irrigation schemes
were instituted. Agriculture, horticulture, and animal hus-
bandry were encouraged and developed, for Uzziah "loved
the soil" (2 Chronicles 26:10). This ensured a steady flow
along the supply lines to his troops.

He built up the defensive forces of the nation and raised
an elite army of 307,500 "who could wage war with great
power" (2 Chronicles 26:13). With such an army, led by
2,600 seasoned officers, he had at his disposal a powerful
striking force. His inventive genius found expression in
secret missiles, "engines of war . . . for the purpose of
shooting arrows and great stones" (2 Chronicles 26:15). He
became one of the most powerful monarchs of his day, and
"his fame extended to the border of Egypt, for he became
very strong" (2 Chronicles 26:8).

The outstanding characteristic of Uzziah's reign was its
unbroken success and prosperity. But the secret lay elsewhere than in his military genius and administrative skill.
It came from the help he received from God. The key to his
success is summed up in eight words: "He was marvelously helped until he was strong" (2 Chronicles 26:15), a verse
that has been the epitaph of many another successful
Christian worker.

There are few who can carry a full cup with a steady
hand. We would do well to pray, "Lord, give us no more

prosperity than You see we can carry with humility," for while adversity has slain its thousands, prosperity has slain its tens of thousands.

Pride Goes Before a Fall

An ominous note creeps into Uzziah's success story: "But when he became strong, his heart was so proud that he acted corruptly" (2 Chronicles 26:16). Unbroken success had eroded personal character. He became obsessed with his own greatness and intoxicated with his success. Prosperity turned his heart away from the God who gave it to him. He forgot the counsel Solomon recorded in Proverbs 8:15, "By me kings reign, and rulers decree justice." God can entrust only few with signal success, because most of us do not carry sufficient spiritual ballast.

Pride is one of the seven deadly sins. Theophylact termed it the citadel and summit of all evil. Pride caused the downfall of Lucifer, the essence of whose sin was trying to establish a kingdom of his own, in independence of God. His was the self-sufficiency that will settle for nothing less than complete independence. It tries to enthrone itself at the expense of God, and no sin is more hateful and abhorrent to Him. There is no point of meeting between a proud heart and God. It was pride that reduced the mighty Nebuchadnezzar to the level of the beasts. It was pride that turned the prosperous Uzziah into a loathsome leper.

Paul had reason to thank God for the painful "thorn in the flesh" (2 Corinthians 12:7) that God caused to afflict him lest he be overwhelmed with pride and self-glory. This uniquely gifted man had been granted unusual and ecstatic experiences that exposed him to extreme temptation to pride, and his own statement acknowledged that he was very conscious of the possibility of succumbing to it. "Because of the surpassing greatness of the revelations," he wrote, "for this reason, to keep me from exalting myself, there was given me a thorn in the flesh, a messenger of Satan to buffet me—to keep me from exalting myself!" (2 Corinthians 12:7).

Nothing so tends to inflate a man with the sense of his

own importance as does the possession of great gifts, or authority, or achievement. And nothing disqualifies him from usefulness more completely than spiritual pride. In Paul's case God brought an equalizing factor into his life lest his ministry be spoiled. At first he viewed it as a crippling handicap from which he struggled to escape. Later, when he saw it in true perspective, he came to regard it as a heavenly advantage.

The Sacrilege of the King

The growing pride of Uzziah led him to attribute his success to his own astuteness and ability, and he neglected to give God the glory. So arrogant and self-reliant did he become that he even had the temerity to intrude into the office of high priest. Like Cain, he had the effrontery to exercise the right to worship God without mediator or atoning sacrifice, the very sin that had brought condign judgment on Korah and his accomplices (Numbers 16:8-10).

On that occasion they were reminded of the Lord's decree that "no layman who is not of the descendants of Aaron should come near to burn incense before the LORD" (Numbers 16:40). In Egypt and in other Middle Eastern nations, the king frequently took part in the religious rites and offered sacrifices, but in Israel the offices of king and priest were kept strictly separate. The dual office of the priest-king Melchizedek, which office foreshadowed the reign of Christ as King-Priest, had no parallel in the Levitical ritual. Uzziah, however, desired to emulate the other Eastern kings in the matter of religion.

Because his reign had been so successful and glorious, Uzziah presumed to think that he had the right to become spiritual head of the nation as well. "His heart was so proud that he acted corruptly, and he was unfaithful to the Lord his God, for he entered the temple of the Lord to burn incense on the altar of incense" (2 Chronicles 26:16).

The godly youth was becoming a megalomaniac. Without doubt he had often read and probably prayed David's prayer, "Keep back Thy servant from presumptuous sins;

let them not rule over me" (Psalm 19:13). But that prayer was no longer on his lips.

Even as old John Knox withstood the arrogance of Queen Mary, a shocked but courageous Azariah with eighty valiant priests attempted to restrain the king in his folly and sacrifice, but pride was now in full control. Uzziah would brook no opposition. With smoking censer swinging, he brushed aside those who attempted to make him desist. Knowing that he was taking his life in his hands, Azariah cried out, "It is not for you, Uzziah, to burn incense to the Lord, but for the priests, the sons of Aaron who are consecrated to burn incense. Get out of the sanctuary, for you have been unfaithful, and will have no honor from the Lord God. But Uzziah . . . was enraged" (2 Chronicles 26:18-19). He went with incense into the place where blood was needed.

The King Becomes a Leper

God is long-suffering and merciful, but there are prescribed limits beyond which, if a man presumes to go, judgment is the inevitable result. Uzziah chose to flout the divine prohibition, and he had to bear the consequences. We cannot presume on the patience of God. For his act of flagrant presumption, the king received a stroke of sudden judgment.

"While he was enraged with the priests, the leprosy broke out on his forehead; . . . and they hurried him out of there, and he himself also hastened to get out because the Lord had smitten him" (2 Chronicles 26:19-20). The king saw the hand of God in the act of judgment. Now he was completely cut off from the house of God. He could not even go as a worshiper.

Where now were his royal pomp and splendor? A leper! Unclean, unclean! He had refused to judge himself, so God had judged him (1 Corinthians 11:31). It was unthinkable that a leper should sit on the throne of David; so he was removed, and his son Jotham ascended the throne. Uzziah could no longer live in the royal palace; so until his death he lived in a segregated house, or hospital.

Miriam had been smitten with the same disease because she presumed to criticize the leaders God had appointed, but her disease was cured in answer to Moses' prayer (Numbers 12:1-15). Nebuchadnezzar was for a season deprived of his reason as a judgment on his pride, but on repentance he was restored to his throne (Daniel 3:1-7; 4:28-37). The tragedy of Uzziah's life is that there is no evidence of repentance, and he was never restored. "King Uzziah was a leper to the day of his death" (2 Chronicles 26:21). He was even denied the burial of a king. The corpse of a leper must not corrupt the tombs of the kings. "They buried him with his fathers in the field of the grave which belonged to the kings, for they said, 'He is a leper' " (2 Chronicles 26:23).

The next chapter introduces a happier note. Uzziah's son Jotham, who succeeded him, "did right in the sight of the Lord, according to all that his father Uzziah had done. . . . Jotham became mighty because he ordered his ways before the Lord" (2 Chronicles 27:2-6).

12

Nehemiah

Nonconformist and Stirrer

"But I did not do so because of the fear of God" (Nehemiah 5:15).

> He [Nehemiah] has never had justice done him in popular estimation. He is not one of the well-known biblical examples of heroic self-abandonment; but he did just what Moses did, and the eulogium of the Epistle to the Hebrews fits him as well as the lawgiver; for he too chose "rather to suffer with the people of God than to enjoy pleasures for a season." So must we all, in our several ways, do, if we would have a share in building the walls of the city of God.[1]
>
> (Alexander Maclaren)

The naive egotism of Nehemiah's autobiographical narrative makes it distinctive among the books of the Bible. But it is the naiveté of an utterly sincere and straightforward man whose egotism is balanced by his recognition of the good hand of God upon him. There is not a touch of gray in the picture; all is in black and white. The story is told with bluntness and extreme factuality. Everything is

1. Alexander Maclaren, *Expositions of Holy Scripture*, 17 vols. (Grand Rapids: Eerdmans, 1944), 3:329.

graphic and vivid, and it leaves the impression of a man of deep conviction, deep devotion, and unusual courage.

It is a sad commentary on the perilous condition of the Hebrew people at Nehemiah's stage in their history that neither king nor prophet nor priest was available to lift the nation from the morass into which it had fallen. The professionals had failed, so to achieve His purpose of blessing for His people God turned to an ordinary citizen who had won his way into a position of trust in the court of a pagan king. God will not be defeated by human failure; He will devise some other method of achieving His plan.

In the providence of God, Nehemiah, the son of Hacaliah, had been reared in exile from his native land and had risen to the position of cupbearer to the king of Persia. From the tenor of Nehemiah's life, the presumption is that he had been brought up and instructed by God-fearing parents.

The office of cupbearer to the king should not be thought of as that of a glorified drink-waiter. It was a lucrative post and was considered one of the most honorable and confidential positions at the court. It admitted Nehemiah into the king's presence on terms of familiarity, though not of equality. The king spoke to him as an intimate rather than as an inferior. Persian monarchs were served by a number of cupbearers, probably as a safety measure, since they were constantly in danger of being poisoned. Each cupbearer served for four months at a time, a fact that made it possible for Nehemiah to be granted leave. It is clear that Nehemiah stood high in the esteem of the king. It was his faithfulness in the discharge of his secular duties that won for him the privileges he later sought. Godliness is not necessarily incompatible with earthly success.

Twelve years previous, Ezra had returned with 1,750 men and their dependents to rebuild Jerusalem, but they had been stopped from completing the task by royal decree, and the city remained largely in ruins. Nehemiah's brother Hanani, with some other Hebrew men, visited him in the palace at Susa, the capital of the kingdom. Like the patriot he was, Nehemiah eagerly enquired about the condition of the Jews who had survived the captivity and about the state of Jerusalem itself.

A Depressing Report

The depressing report the men brought weighed heavily on Nehemiah's spirits. "When I heard these words, I sat down and wept and mourned for days; and I was fasting and praying before the God of heaven" (Nehemiah 1:4).

There was abundant cause for his concern. The people had become decadent and hopeless. The economy was in ruins; the city walls were broken down, and its gates were burned. It was in this impossible situation that Nehemiah discerned a supreme challenge to faith—and accepted it.

His prayers and tears were a reflection of his own devotional life. The true man is revealed when he is on his knees. He is what he is when he is alone with God—and no more. Tears are often the mark of power, not of weakness, and Nehemiah was no weakling. Patriotism and concern for the glory of God and the blessing of His people inspired his prayers. The prayer of Nehemiah 1:5-11 is a blending of reverence, confession, contrition, and confidence. He held God to His covenant and to His plighted Word as a reason to grant him success in his approach to the king for permission to rebuild Jerusalem's walls. He saw clearly that if the city was to be restored as the center of national life and worship, this was the first essential.

So deeply was Nehemiah affected by the plight of his people that his evident concern caused the king to ask him, "Why is your face sad though you are not sick? This is nothing but sadness of heart" (Nehemiah 2:2). Now for an official to look sad in the king's presence or to seek permission to leave the court was a breach of etiquette punishable by death. Little wonder that Nehemiah "was very much afraid" (Nehemiah 2:2). With an upward look to heaven, he made his request, fully aware of how risky it was to display interest in a city that had come under royal displeasure.

God honored Nehemiah's faith. The king not only granted him the desired vacation, but he also provided the timber necessary for the restoration of gates and houses. Nehemiah's prayers and tears had not been in vain. The pagan king knew nothing of the forces released by his cupbearer's prayers.

Three days after arriving in Jerusalem, with characteristic caution Nehemiah stole out at night to reconnoiter and see for himself the state of the walls and the magnitude of the task (Nehemiah 2:11-16). He did not make the mistake of taking precipitate action before he had formulated his plans.

Next he encouraged the dispirited people by recounting how the favor of God had moved the king to grant the needed permission and provision. His faith and zeal were so infectious that despite the opposition of the neighboring peoples they responded, "Let us arise and build" (Nehemiah 2:18). The remainder of the story provides a noble example of inspired and charismatic leadership.

Prayer Fundamental, Not Supplemental

The outstanding impression of Nehemiah's artless story is that of a man to whom prayer was fundamental, not supplemental. It was not a mere addendum to his work; his work grew out of his praying. It is evident that he was no stranger at the throne of grace. His prayers were not merely for set seasons; they were an integral part of his daily life and work (see Nehemiah 1:4, 6; 2:4; 4:4, 9; 5:19; 6:14; 13:14, 22, 29).

It is instructive too, to note the part prayer played in the reconstruction of the city. Prayer secured the king's favor and cooperation. It obtained the necessary supplies and protection. It endowed Nehemiah with courage and wisdom in dealing with adversaries. It imparted to him business shrewdness and tact in adjusting problems of labor and wages. It equipped him to deal with wily and crafty officials. It afforded him peace in the midst of slander and lies. It renewed his faith and optimism.

Nehemiah displayed great courage in the face of danger and opposition. When urged to take sanctuary in the Temple behind closed doors to escape a death threat, he displayed a fearlessness that further strengthened his grip on the people's hearts and raised their morale. With fine scorn he responded: "Should a man like me flee? And could one such as I go into the temple to save his life? I will not go in" (Nehemiah 6:11).

Genuine concern for the welfare of his people pervades the whole narrative, a concern so obvious that it disturbed his adversaries. "When Sanballat the Horonite and Tobiah the Ammonite official heard about it, it was very displeasing to them that someone had come to seek the welfare of the sons of Israel" (Nehemiah 2:10). He identified with his people not only in their sorrows and sufferings, but also in their national sins—"the sins of the sons of Israel which we have sinned against Thee; I and my father's house have sinned" (Nehemiah 1:6).

Nehemiah displayed empathy to a marked degree. He was always willing to lend a sympathetic ear to the problems and grievances of the people, and where necessary he took prompt remedial measures (Nehemiah 4:10-14; 5:1-13). A Christian leader once said to the author, concerning someone who had come to him in justifiable distress, "I wasn't going to have him weeping on my shoulder." But that is what the shoulder of the leader is for!

Secrets of Success

Throughout Nehemiah's bold activities there ran a wholesome strain of caution. On reaching Jerusalem, he did not rush into feverish activity. "So I came to Jerusalem and was there three days," the record runs (Nehemiah 2:11). Only after appraising the situation did he act. Even his reconnaissance was done in strict secrecy under cover of night. Knowing the danger of sharing plans with too many people, he did not tell anyone what God was putting into his mind to do (Nehemiah 2:12).

Quick and clear decision marked his activities. He did not defer for future consideration what called for prompt action. To this energetic and disciplined man, procrastination was anathema. But his decisions were strictly impartial. When they deserved it, the nobles and rulers received his censure just as freely as did the common people. "I . . . contended with the nobles and the rulers and said to them. . . . Therefore, I held a great assembly against them" (Nehemiah 5:7). There was no respect of persons. Every man had to pull his own weight. Workers were drawn from all classes, women as well as men.

Nehemiah's character combined true spiritual-mindedness with an earthy realism. His spiritual approach to problems did not preclude a realistic facing of hard facts. "We prayed to our God, and because of them we set up a guard against them day and night" (Nehemiah 4:9)—an old version of the later "Trust in God and keep your powder dry." He displayed neither a presumptuous independence of God nor a rash neglect of adequate preparation.

In accepting responsibility for the rebuilding operation, Nehemiah did not evade its more onerous implications; rather, he carried his assignment through to a successful conclusion despite difficulties and dangers. There was no thought of turning back. In discharging this obligation, he renounced rights that were his as leader. In proof of his disinterestedness, he was able to say, "From the day that I was appointed to be their governor, . . . neither I nor my kinsmen have eaten the governor's food allowance. But the former governors who were before me laid burdens on the people and took from them bread and wine besides forty shekels of silver. . . . But I did not do so because of the fear of God" (Nehemiah 5:14-15).

Nehemiah emerges as a man calm in crisis, vigorous in administration, fearless in danger, courageous in decision, thorough in organization, vigilant against intrigue, disinterested in leadership—an altogether remarkable man. He was humble enough to attribute his success to the good hand of God upon him.

Successful Strategy

The methods Nehemiah adopted to secure maximum co-operation from the whole group have much to teach us. To have the wall rebuilt within fifty-two days was a remarkable tribute to the success of his strategy.

1. He aimed to *raise the morale* of his colleagues—an important function of the responsible leader. He achieved this by stimulating their faith and directing their thoughts away from the magnitude of their problems and to the greatness of God. Faith begets faith. Pessimism begets unbelief. It is the primary function of the leader to feed faith to his colleagues. Scattered throughout the record are faith-begetting assurances. "The God of heaven will give us success" (Nehemiah 2:20). "Do not be afraid of them; remember the Lord who is great and awesome" (Nehemiah 4:14). "Our God will fight for us" (Nehemiah 4:20). "The joy of the Lord is your strength" (Nehemiah 8:10).

2. He was *generous* both *in appreciation and in encouragement*. Coming to a demoralized and discouraged people, his first objective was to kindle hope and secure cooperation. This he did by recounting the good hand of God upon his endeavors and by sharing with the people his vision and utter confidence in God (Nehemiah 2:18, 20).

3. While faults and failings must be recognized and corrected, the manner in which it is done is of great importance. Nehemiah had the knack—or was it the result of thought and self-discipline?—of doing it in such a way as to inspire people to do better. His *firm, impartial discipline* won their continued confidence and further established his authority.

4. He *did not allow potential causes of discontent to develop*, but dealt with them promptly. Two typical cases are recorded. At one point the people were discouraged by weariness and obstruction (Nehemiah 4:10-16). They were desperately tired and exhausted. Accumulated rubbish impeded their progress. They were being intimidated by their enemies. What tactics did Nehemiah adopt? He directed their thoughts to God (Nehemiah 4:14), but he also saw that they were adequately armed (Nehemiah 4:16). Then he regrouped them and deployed them at strategic points. He harnessed the strength of the family unit and ordered half the people to work while the other half either rested or maintained the defense. Once they saw that their

leader appreciated their problem and was grappling with it, courage and optimism returned.

The second problem arose because the people were disillusioned through the greed and heartlessness of their own brethren (Nehemiah 5:1-15). The lands of the poorer people were mortgaged to the hilt, and some of their children were sold into slavery. Nothing so affects the morale of a people as when the welfare of their children is adversely affected. Again Nehemiah's tactics were exemplary.

He listened attentively to their complaints and sympathized with them in their dilemma. He trounced and shamed the nobles for their heartlessness in exacting high rates of interest from their kinsmen (Nehemiah 5:7), and he contrasted their actions with his own altruism (Nehemiah 5:14-15). He appealed for immediate restitution to be made. So great was his morale and spiritual ascendancy that they replied, "We will give it back and will require nothing from them; we will do exactly as you say" (Nehemiah 5:12).

5. In company with his colleague Ezra, Nehemiah *restored the authority of the Word of God* in the nation (Nehemiah 8:1-8). But for this factor, the reforms which he instituted would have been short-lived or even impossible. He vigorously enforced the standards of the Word of God, and this imparted spiritual authority to his actions.

The Feast of Tabernacles, which had not been kept since Joshua's day, was once more observed. How the work-weary people must have reveled in the week-long holiday and festivities! The regular reading of the Scripture induced repentance and confession of sin on the part of both priests and people (Nehemiah 9:3-5).

6. Nehemiah *cleansed the Temple* of Tobiah's sacrilegious furniture (Nehemiah 13:4-9). In achieving his ends, he was not averse to adopting muscular methods. "It was very displeasing to me, so I threw all of Tobiah's household goods out of the room" (Nehemiah 13:8). The holy vessels were restored, and tithes were once again brought to the treasury (Nehemiah 13:9, 12). The Sabbath was enforced, and intermarriage with the surrounding nations was forbidden (Nehemiah 13:15, 23-28).

7. He displayed considerable *administrative and orga-*

nizational skill. Before formulating detailed plans, he conducted a careful survey and made a detailed assessment of the personnel available. He did not neglect the unglamorous paperwork. He did his homework. Each group was entrusted with a specific and clearly defined area of responsibility. He gave adequate recognition to subordinate leaders, mentioning them by name, thus giving them the feeling that they were more than mere cogs in a machine.

8. He recognized the importance of *delegation of responsibility.* "I put Hanani my brother, and Hananiah the commander of the fortress, in charge of Jerusalem, for he was a faithful man and feared God more than many" (Nehemiah 7:2). He thus had reason to justify his nepotism. By this delegation of responsibility, he not only lightened his own burden, but also he gave other able men the chance to develop their leadership potential.

9. *The way in which he met organized opposition* has valuable contemporary lessons. The opposition took various forms: insult (Nehemiah 2:19; 4:23); innuendo (Nehemiah 2:19); infiltration (Nehemiah 4:11; 6:10-13); intimidation (Nehemiah 6:1-9); intrigue (Nehemiah 4:7-8). To steer a steady course amid those swirling currents required more than human wisdom, and Nehemiah knew where to obtain it. He consistently resorted to prayer. When it was safe to do so, he ignored his adversaries, refusing to allow them to deflect him from his goal. "I am doing a great work and I cannot come down" (Nehemiah 6:3). But when it was prudent, he took all necessary precautionary measures (Nehemiah 4:16).

In review, the achievements of this rugged and blunt man are amazing. Not only did he rebuild the wall of the city in eight weeks, but over the period of his governorship, thirteen years, he changed the whole face of the nation. He augmented the population of the city (Nehemiah 11:1). He restored Temple worship and the supremacy of the Word of God. He ended oppressive moneylending and redeemed large numbers of slaves. He stopped marriages with Gentiles and enforced strict Sabbath observance. Characteristically, he closed his autobiography with a prayer, "Remember me, O my God, for good" (Nehemiah 13:31).

NEW TESTAMENT

13

Andrew

An Ordinary Man?

"He found first his own brother Simon" (John 1:41).

Most of Christ's followers must remain unknown to fame. They must live a simple life, a thing of routine. Few take notice of us. Thus we live day by day, not idly or unprofitably, indeed, but in a small place—until the end comes. . . . Such is the life and lot of the majority.[1]

(John A. Hutton)

"An ordinary man." "He never made the front rank." "He was in no sense a great man." "A pattern Christian." Such are varying appraisals of Andrew, son of Jonas of Bethsaida. He was brother to Simon Peter, and he became the patron saint of Scotland, Russia, and Greece. This latter fact throws an interesting light on the character of the man. The truth or otherwise of the above assessments will emerge as we study the twelve references to the apostle in the New Testament.

The twelve apostles appear in the gospels in three groups of four. Andrew is uniformly in the first group,

1. In Ralph Gale Turnbull, "Andrew: A Pattern Christian," *Moody Monthly,* October 1940, p. 65.

along with James, John, and Peter. The order of the names varies, but none of the first group appears in either of the others. Andrew was not, however, included in the inner circle of intimates of Jesus who experienced the glory of the transfiguration and witnessed the poignancy of the Gethsemane prayers. He never attained the eminence of his more flamboyant brother, but that did not prevent his commonplace ministry from putting the whole church deeply in his debt. He apparently lived with Peter, who was his partner in business (Mark 1:29).

The first great crisis of his life occurred when he came under the austere preaching of John the Baptist, who was calling apostate Israel to repentance. The response to his preaching had been ovwhelming, and Andrew and his companion were caught up in the new spiritual movement. They saw Jesus' baptism, and the next day they heard the prophet's startling announcement: "Behold, the Lamb of God!"—words that identified Him as the long-awaited Messiah (John 1:35-37, 40).

For Andrew it was a day of destiny. It had begun like every other day, but for him life could never be the same again. "One of the two who heard John speak, and followed [Jesus], was Andrew" (John 1:40). It was a case of love at first sight, and throughout his life his devotion never waned, his following never faltered. In this incident there is a fine though indirect tribute to John: his testimony inevitably led to Jesus. His ministry was Christ-centered.

A Fisher of Men

It was not long before Andrew was confronted with a challenge that tested both his dedication and his motivation. As Jesus was walking along the shore of the Sea of Galilee, His discerning eye rested on two industrious fishermen. He had been praying for His Father's guidance in the selection of the men to be the instruments of His world-purpose. Immediately when He saw Simon Peter and Andrew He sensed the Spirit's inner witness that they were to be the first of that privileged company. " 'Follow me,' " He said, " 'and I will make you fishers of men.' And they immediately left the nets, and followed Him" (Matthew 4:19-20).

The operative words in our Lord's call were, "I will make you." There are no self-made workers in His Kingdom. Henceforth Andrew was to come under Jesus' personal instruction and supervision. The Lord took Andrew's natural gifts and abilities as they were expressed in his normal occupation and redirected them into spiritual channels. That is the Great Teacher's usual, though not exclusive, method. When the gifts of nature are consecrated to His service, "the natural craft of the earthly endowment becomes consecrated skill in the spiritual order."[2]

That Andrew did indeed become a successful fisher of men as Jesus had promised is borne out by the fact that on each of the three occasions in which he figured prominently, he was engaged in introducing others to Jesus.

Andrew was one of those godly men who were "looking for the consolation of Israel" (Luke 2:25), but he nevertheless shared the narrow and insular outlook of his fellows. They were all in the grip of Jewish prejudices and animosities, and their subsequent actions revealed their tendency to be bigoted and racially exclusive. There were many lessons they had to learn in the school of Christ in coming days. Before they graduated they would have to submit to a stringent and demanding educational process.

The First Lesson

Andrew received his first major lesson in a never-to-be-forgotten private session with Jesus. He and his companion (was it John?) had heard the Baptist's cry, "Behold, the Lamb of God" (John 1:36) and had been irresistibly drawn by His magnetic personality. Curiosity mingled with wistfulness caused them to follow Him.

With characteristic clarity of decision, Andrew switched his allegiance from John the Baptist to the One to whom John pointed. This was not the easy decision of a fickle

2. Ibid., p. 66.

man, but the irreversible choice of conviction. There was an aura about Jesus that awakened confidence. There began to dawn on Andrew the suspicion that this might be the Messiah.

On seeing the two men following Him, Jesus took the initiative and encouraged them with the kindly enquiry, "What do you seek?" (John 1:38). Their timid reply indicated a hunger for more intimate contact with the new Teacher. "Where are You staying?" they enquired (John 1:38). "Come, and you will see" (John 1:39) was the cordial response—a tacit invitation to stay and visit with Him. What a unique privilege for the favored two!

If John is using the Roman calculation of time in his record, as is most likely, the hour of their encounter would have been four o'clock in the afternoon. "Coming to Jesus in the late afternoon and then having the kind conversation that the circumstances indicate," writes Leon Morris, "almost requires us to understand 'abode' [John 1:39, KJV] as 'remained overnight.' "[3]

What intimacies, what precious truths Jesus must have shared with His new friends on that memorable night. In His sympathetic presence it would be easy for them to open their hearts and pour out their eager questions. The details we shall never know, but the impact of that interview was immediately apparent. Without delay Andrew burst in on his brother with an excited, "We have found the Messiah" (John 1:41). Nothing would do but that he must come and meet Jesus—a meeting that proved epoch-making for both the church and the world.

The Thrill of Discovery

Is it not significant that the first disciple to follow Jesus was the first to bring his own brother to the Christ? The thrill of his newfound discovery left Andrew no option but

3. Leon Morris, *The Gospel According to John*, The New International Commentary on the New Testament (Grand Rapids: Eerdmans, 1971), p. 158.

to share it with his own immediate family circle—by no means the easiest sphere of witness. Indeed, the most searching test of discipleship is often encountered in the family circle, where we are so well known and where inconsistencies of our lives can neutralize our testimonies.

Andrew "found first his own brother Simon" (John 1:41), who in the providence of God would far outshine his more pedestrian brother. What was it that convinced Peter, too, that Jesus was the Messiah? Is it fanciful to suppose that during those hours of intercourse with Jesus some of His radiance had rubbed off on Andrew and that the change in him convinced Peter that here was no ordinary man?

While Peter attained great prominence as the leader of the apostolic band, the great preacher at Pentecost, and later the New Testament writer, it must not be forgotten that it was Andrew who was God's messenger to introduce Peter to Jesus. Andrew was dwarfed by Peter's massive personality and was known as "Simon Peter's brother," but no fisher of men made a more influential and important catch than he. Archbishop William Temple considered Andrew's action as great a service to the church as any man ever rendered.

It was an obscure Sunday school teacher who won Moody to Christ. An unlettered man with a repetitious sermon brought Spurgeon to Christ. Andrew's winning of his brother was authentic evidence of his possession of new life in Christ. "Let them first learn to practice piety in regard to their own family" (1 Timothy 5:4) is a sound principle for new disciples. Andrew did not argue and debate with Peter; he simply bore testimony to his own experience of Christ. This is still one of the most effective and persuasive methods of fishing for men.

A Second Lesson

The next crisis in Andrew's educative process arose out of the miracle of the feeding of the five thousand (John 6:1-14). The Lord's compassionate concern for the crowds who followed Him forbade His sending them away hungry, as His disciples had suggested. The resulting emergency provided a new lesson in faith. "Jesus . . . said to Philip, 'Where are we to buy bread, that these may eat?' *And this He was saying to test him*" (John 6:5-6, italics added)—and to test the other disciples too. How would they react? Philip treated it purely as a matter of economics, made a swift calculation, and dismissed it as impossible. "Two hundred denarii worth of bread is not sufficient for them, for every one to receive a little" (John 6:7). He could assess the magnitude of the problem, but he could not provide a solution.

Philip and the other disciples saw a difficulty in the opportunity. Andrew discerned an opportunity in the difficulty. That is the hallmark of the man of faith. Most of us are more competent in assessing the magnitude of the problem than in providing a solution through our faith. Andrew's faith was only tentative and timid, but it was sufficient to stir him to positive action.

While Philip and the others argued among themselves, Andrew was pursuing independent inquiries, and he came up with a suggestion: "There is a lad here, who has five barley loaves, and two fish." Then, overcome again with the ludicrous inadequacy of the supply, his faith faltered, and he added, "But what are these for so many people?" (John 6:9).

Andrew was a cautious man. Had he been too rash in even advancing the suggestion? But in spite of the human improbability of the situation, his confidence in Jesus was sufficiently strong to cause him to introduce the lad to Jesus. If He were indeed the Messiah, might he not be able to do the impossible? In the event, he learned that divine power works through inadequate and unlikely means when they are handed over to Him.

Of the whole group, Andrew was the only one who seemed to evince the slightest faith in the ability of the Master to resolve the impossible situation. And what of the boy? Would he ever be likely to forget the Man who multiplied his lunch five thousand times? Would he be less drawn to Him than Andrew had been? It is possible that this lad's soul was added to Andrew's catch.

We Would See Jesus

Andrew's next appearance in the Scripture record occurs when some Greeks were making a pilgrimage to Jerusalem to worship at the feast (John 12:20-26). Word of the new Teacher's astounding activities had kindled in their hearts a desire to know more about Him. Accosting Philip, they said, "Sir, we wish to see Jesus" (John 12:21). Characteristically, Philip was uncertain of what to do. They might want to see Jesus, but would He want to see them? In Philip's favor it must be remembered that Jesus had said, "I was sent only to the lost sheep of the house of Israel" (Matthew 15:24).

In his perplexity, Philip brought his problem to Andrew; the act was thus a tribute to the latter's sound judgment. Andrew did not share Philip's doubt. The memory of the heartwarming reception Jesus had accorded him was still fresh in Andrew's mind. He was confident of Christ's willingness to meet those who came to Him with inquiring hearts. So in company with Philip he introduced the Greek inquirers to Jesus. It was a significant occasion, and it may well be that it was Andrew, not Paul, who saw the first signs of the ingathering of the Gentiles. "Jesus was the Saviour of the world and this group of Gentiles symbolically represents the world seeking its salvation from Jesus."[4]

It should be noted, too, that it was Andrew's spiritual insight in introducing the Greeks to Jesus that drew from Him the parable of the grain of wheat, with its preview of the ultimate worldwide harvest in the Kingdom (John 12:24).

The last recorded incident in Andrew's career introduces another facet of his character—an inquiring mind. It was one of the occasions when he was associated with his three friends in an intimate session with the Master (Mark 13:1-4). His ministry was drawing to a close, and as the apostolic band moved away from the Temple, one of their number drew His attention to its massive and magni-

4. Ibid., p. 592.

ficent stones. To their amazement, Jesus responded by predicting the destruction of the Temple. "Do you see these great buildings? Not one stone shall be left upon another which will not be torn down" (Mark 13:2).

That revolutionary statement stirred the disciples to discussion and inquiry. Andrew and his companions had good reason to fear lest the Lord's words be interpreted as treason—as indeed later became the case. What did His cryptic statement mean? The four men decided to take their problem to Jesus privately. They were interested in the timing of this and related events. "Tell us, when will these things be, and what will be the sign of Your coming, and of the end of the age?" (Matthew 24:3). Their question opened the way for Christ's great prophetic pronouncement that is the key to all unfulfilled prophecy. He has the answer and will respond to all sincere questions.

The last glimpse we have of Andrew is in the sacred upper room where, with the others, he was awaiting the promised Pentecostal Gift. "These all with one mind were continually devoting themselves to prayer, along with the women, and Mary the mother of Jesus, and with His brothers" (Acts 1:14). Obedient to the Lord's command, he participated in the Pentecostal effusion, in the power of which his first convert preached a sermon that brought three thousand souls to the Savior.

An Assessment of Character

With these incidents before us, we are now in a position to make an assessment of Andrew's character. Although he was the same stock as Peter, seldom have brothers been less alike in temperament. If Peter was the typical voluble extremist, Andrew was the typical *cautious conservative*. It was not without reason that Scotland adopted Andrew and not Peter as patron saint!

But the conservative temperament has its own built-in weaknesses. An excess of caution tends to discourage taking fresh initiatives; it settles for precedent rather than adventure. An old divine voiced a typical conservative outlook when he declared that if he had ever, under God, been instrumental in accomplishing any good, it had been by "holding back."[5] This genus is not extinct.

One of the author's friends, a man who has great achievements to his credit in a position of strategic importance in the evangelical world, on reviewing his life was surprised to discover that his greatest mistakes had been made as a result of lack of venturesomeness. That is one of the dangers of the cautious conservative.

As to *motivation*, Andrew was no ambitious place-seeker. He was one of that rare breed of men who have mastered the delicate art of playing second fiddle well. His modest acceptance of a role subordinate to his brilliant brother speaks well of his humility. Throughout the record there is no suggestion of a desire for the limelight, nor is there any evidence of a desire to displace Peter.

It could not have been easy to be known merely as Simon Peter's brother, as many another brother has discovered. Most of us want recognition in our own right. Nor could it have been enjoyable for him to feel that he had fallen short of the intimacy with Jesus enjoyed by his three friends. He belonged to the elect company who qualify for the eulogy "He who rules his spirit, [is better] than he who captures a city" (Proverbs 16:32). He was content just to be himself, an ordinary man.

The *power of clear decision* was another quality Andrew exhibited. He had no difficulty in making up his mind, once he was sure of his facts; and having made a decision, he allowed no turning back. When John the Baptist identified Jesus as the Messiah, Andrew lost no time in following Him. When Jesus later called him, personally, without argument or delay Andrew left his nets and followed Him. When Philip approached him with the tricky problem of the Greek enquirers, Andrew promptly took them to Jesus. When the crisis arose with the hungry crowds, Andrew alone took decisive action. He was a man of clear decision.

Nor was he lacking in *moral courage*. At the very begin-

5. James I. Vance, *The College of Apostles* (New York: Revell, 1935), p. 27.

ning of his discipleship he evidenced this quality by wit-
nessing in his family circle, admittedly one of the most
difficult places to do so. It has been suggested that he was
clannish in thinking first of his own family; but was that
not his first responsibility, as it is ours? He must share his
great discovery, and who had a better claim than his own
brother and business partner?

He displayed considerable courage, too, in sponsoring
the Greek enquirers when they sought an interview with
Jesus. He knew that his orthodox brethren regarded the
Greeks as "gentile dogs," and in identifying with them he
was running in the face of bitter racial prejudice. But to
him loyalty to Jesus now meant more than the disapproval
of his peers. He was prepared to be misjudged as he plowed
a new furrow—that of recognizing the despised Gentiles
as possible recipients of divine grace.

If tradition can be trusted, Andrew demonstrated great
courage in taking the good news to the barbarous Scyth-
ians, of whom Josephus said that they differed little from
wild beasts. Yet Andrew introduced these unpromising
disciples to Jesus. Tradition also has it that he was put to
death in Achaia, nailed to the cross with arms of equal
length that bears his name, St. Andrew's cross.

Was Andrew an ordinary man? Yes, but he was a man
whose influence is abiding because of his love and loyalty
to Christ. He was an ordinary man of average capacity; he
was without outstanding gifts; but he was of sterling character. Though he had no earthshaking achievements to his
credit, through his faithful witness and self-effacing service he left his mark on succeeding ages. The world needs
more such ordinary men.

14

Thomas

Doubter Turned Confessor

"I will not believe. . . . My Lord and my God!" (John 20:25, 28).

Of all the Master's men, Thomas is the one to whom least jutice is commonly done. He is, in fact, mostly known for what are felt to be his faults. When his name is mentioned it is usually as "doubting Thomas" that he is identified. As such he might be held in a certain degree of wondering disrespect, not to say contempt, had not the Resurrection story, in which he and the Master figure together, been chronicled.[1]

(J. Stuart Holden)

In our day of endemic doubt and cynicism, many will be encouraged by the fact that among His twelve carefully selected disciples, Jesus included one whose name has become a synonym for doubt. Can we doubt that one of the reasons for the choice was that in succeeding generations other disciples who are plagued with doubt might find timely help?

How should we remember Thomas: as the lugubrious

1. J. Stuart Holden, *The Master and His Men* (London: Marshall, Morgan & Scott, 1953), p. 94.

doubter or as the rapturous confessor? We have a clue in our Lord's attitude to people. When Andrew introduced Peter to Him, His first words were: "You are Simon; . . . you shall be called Cephas (which translated means Peter)" (John 1:42). You *are*. . . . You *shall be*. Jesus always saw the hidden potential in people.

Hidden Potential

Our Lord's play on Peter's name was not a meaningless joke, but an appraisal and a prophecy. *Cephas* was the Aramaic equivalent of the Greek *Peter*. *Petra* signifies a massive ledge of rock, not a pebble. So in calling Peter "Mr. Rock," Jesus was assuring him that although he was now fickle and unstable, under His molding hand he would develop a character as stable as a rock.

And shall we adopt a less generous attitude in our appraisal of Thomas, the twin? Just as He did to Peter, Jesus might well have said to Thomas, "*You are* temperamentally Thomas, the chronic disbeliever; but under my transforming hand *you will become* Thomas, the peerless confessor."

The picture of Thomas in Scripture is of a typical melancholic: he found it desperately easy to look on the dark side of things and conjure up difficulties. Thomas's nature was set in a minor key. He was inclined to view a gloomy possibility as a certainty. The trust and optimistic outlook of the child was absent from his makeup.

Although he had a warm and passionate heart, it tended to be overridden by the speculative side of his nature, which influenced him toward suspicion and distrust. By nature he was argumentative and demanded a reason for everything. Secondhand evidence was not enough. He was the prudent type of man who would not sign an insurance proposal until he had read all the small print. Add to all this a touch of obstinacy, and you have a temperamental problem on your hands.

Thomas would not have described himself as a doubter or unbeliever, but only as a realist who must be true to himself. And did he not have the right to require satisfying evidence for his beliefs? He felt things deeply, and he was equally vehement in his beliefs and disbeliefs.

Three incidents throw light upon Thomas's temperament and disposition and enable us to interpret with a fair degree of probability the factors that lay behind his entrenched attitude of doubt. On examination, it will be found that the same traits of character are revealed in each incident.

The first was sparked by the Lord's insistence on going to the house of mourning in Bethany in spite of the obvious danger to Himself. The second arose out of Thomas's querulous interruption of the Lord's discourse on the night of the Last Supper. The third was the memorable interview after the resurrection. With this material, let us endeavor to discover the essential personality of the apostle.

The Bethany Incident (John 11:1-16)

The serious illness of Lazarus had created an urgent domestic crisis in the home at Bethany. In full confidence that He would hasten to their side, Martha and Mary dispatched to Jesus a message with an implied appeal for help. On receiving the message, Jesus announced His intention to return to Judea. In the light of His recent danger there, His apprehensive disciples attempted to dissuade Him. "Rabbi," they protested, "the Jews were just now seeking to stone You; and are You going there again?" (John 11:8). In the light of the murderous mood of the authorities, the idea seemed to the disciples to be suicidal madness.

When Jesus persisted in His purpose and said to them, "Let us go to him [Lazarus]" (John 11:15), with characteristic pessimism but also typical devotion "Thomas . . . said to his fellow disciples, 'Let us also go, that we may die with Him' " (John 11:16). He could see only one end to such a foolhardy venture. Doubt has a short memory, and Thomas had forgotten the occasions in the past when Jesus had escaped from His enemies.

But despite his own misgivings, Thomas would be in it with the Master to the end. If He were going to die, He

would not die alone! Perhaps instead of smiling at his pessimism we should be coveting the devotion that was greater than his doubts.

The Upper Room Incident (John 14:1-6)

It was the night of the betrayal, and Jesus was opening
His heart to His beloved men. He was preparing them for
His departure. "If I go and prepare a place for you, I will
come again, and receive you to Myself; that where I am,
there you may be also. And you know the way where I am
going" (John 14:3-4).

Thomas interrupted Him brusquely, "Lord, we do not
know where You are going; how do we know the way?"
(John 14:5). It was as though he were rebuking the Lord
for taking too much for granted. To Thomas, Christ's statement seemed unreasonable, if not untrue, and the reaction was typical of Thomas. How could they know the way
if He had not distinctly told them? Perhaps his outburst
expressed a genuine perplexity, in which he was voicing
the question of the whole group.

Jesus might well have reproved Thomas for his abrupt
interruption; instead, He met him with sympathetic understanding. Moreover, He gave him information for which
he had not asked. We should be grateful to Thomas, for
this incident elicited one of the greatest and most preg-
nant philosophical statements of all times: "Jesus said to
him, 'I am the way, and the truth, and the life; no one
comes to the Father, but through Me' " (John 14:6).

In this statement Jesus claimed to be *the way to God,
the truth about God, and the life of God.* Not only does He
show the way to God, but He *is* the way. Not only does He
teach the truth, He *is* the truth. Not only does He impart
life, He *is* the life.

The Postresurrection Incident (John 20:24-29)

It *would* be Thomas who was the only disciple absent
when the risen Lord burst in on the fearful disciples in the
upper room on that first day of the week! We are not told

why Thomas had chosen to isolate himself, and any suggestion is only a matter of surmise. But knowing what we do of his temperament, and knowing the sequel, we can attempt an intelligent guess. Was he alone somewhere hugging his despair? Was he indulging the luxury of solitary sadness to which the melancholic is prone? Was he despondent over his recent desertion of his Master in His hour of need? Perhaps he was so engulfed in grief that he could not bear to face his more resilient fellows.

Self-imposed Isolation

Whatever the reason, Thomas's self-imposed isolation cost him a sight of his Lord. He missed personally receiving His commission: "As the Father has sent Me, I also send you" (John 20:21). He missed the breath of the Spirit when Jesus "breathed on them, and said to them, 'Receive the Holy Spirit' " (John 20:22).

When his brethren excitedly told him, "We have seen the Lord!" (John 20:25), Thomas was plunged into despondency. Had Jesus left him out? Whatever his thoughts, he burst out, "Unless I shall see in His hands the imprint of the nails, and put my finger into the place of the nails, and put my hand into His side, I will not believe!" (John 20:25). His was not a doubt waiting to be dispelled, but a doubt he was determined to surrender only on his own terms.

Now Thomas was no atheist or agnostic. He was not incredulous of the supernatural. He had shown the reality of his love for Jesus by his willingness to die with Him. The raising of Lazarus had posed no problems for him. He did not absolutely refuse to accept the fact of the resurrection, but he demanded incontrovertible physical evidence before he accepted it.

In sublime condescension, the Lord of glory met the obstinate and gloomy Thomas on his own basis. Once again the disciples were gathered in the upper room. Without warning "Jesus came, the doors having been shut, and stood in their midst" (John 20:26). In an awed hush, Jesus singled out the absentee.

It is a moving fact that the two disciples whom the Lord

favored with special attention after His resurrection were the greatest denier and the greatest doubter. He specialized in mending broken reeds and in fanning dimly burning wicks into flame.

That Jesus knew what Thomas had said became evident when He said to him, "Reach here your finger, and see My hands; and reach here your hand, and put it into My side; and be not unbelieving, but believing" (John 20:27). There was no word of rebuke, only a gentle appeal to have done with the disbelief that was shutting him out of blessing. Jesus discerned behind the exterior of doubt the beating of a loving heart. "Here is the evidence," He seemed to be saying. "Accept it, and renounce your doubts."

"Be not unbelieving" here carries the meaning "*Become* not unbelieving, but believing." The implication is that we can cultivate the habit of either belief or unbelief, for faith involves the activity of the will. Unbelief is fueled by isolating ourselves from fellow believers. Faith is nourished among the believing community with Jesus in the midst. That was where Thomas had made his mistake.

Did Thomas actually touch the sacred wounds on the body of the Master? In the radiant presence of Jesus, did he still demand further evidence? What need of visual and tactile evidence when He was obviously alive and present?

Then the true Thomas asserted himself. Flinging his doubts to the winds, he cast himself at the nail-pierced feet in abject surrender. His incredulity vanished like the morning mist. He took the leap out of doubt into faith; his rapturous confession was: "My Lord and my God!" (John 20:28).

What was it that delivered Thomas from his unbelief? The sight of the risen Savior. One look was sufficient. Before, he had demanded both to see and to feel before he would be satisfied. Now not tangible physical evidence, but the touch of the magnetic personality of the Son of God forever banished his unbelief, and the dismal doubter became the rapturous confessor.

> With what a new-born, deep intensity
> Of consecrated love and quickened trust,

All perfected, the doubting Thomas must
Have loved the comprehending Christ, when He
Looked in his heart, then bade him come and see
The nail-prints in those tender palms, and thrust
Into that blessed side his hand of dust.
Not for the proof vouchsafed so graciously
Must he anew have loved his Lord—ah, no!
That was of all the very smallest part;
Belief, perchance, had dawned ere long, without
A granted sign, to his slow mind; but, O!
The mighty Savior understood his heart,
And had divine compassion on his doubt.[2]

(Katrina Trask)

It is a consoling fact that the confession of the arch-doubter should be the fullest and noblest recorded in Scripture. When he came to faith, the most sublime confession of the ages formulated itself within his loyal heart. The greatest doubter came to the fullest belief.

We are accustomed to magnify his doubt, but what shall we say of his belief? His confession was couched in language possible only to passionate love; it was the language of a man who had endured the agony of doubt and had experienced a complete revulsion of feeling. Jesus had revealed Himself as both omniscient and omnipotent, and Thomas bowed to his sovereign Lord in awe and worship.

The Beatitude of Sightless Faith

Thomas believed because he was presented with the evidence he had demanded, but the Lord was too faithful to allow an important lesson to go unmastered. Very gently Jesus said, "Because you have seen Me, have you believed? Blessed are they who do not see, and yet believed" (John 20:29). Christ stressed the superior blessedness of believing without seeing. "Faith which results from seeing is good; but faith which results from hearing is more excellent."[3]

2. In James I. Vance, *The College of Apostles* (New York: Revell, 1935), p. 77.
3. William Hendriksen, *The Gospel of John*, Geneva Commentary Series (London: Banner of Truth, 1959), 2:466.

There is much we may learn from the experience of
Thomas about the method of the Master with doubting
hearts. No believer is immune to the ravages of doubt.
Even after having genuinely believed, it is still possible to
have intellectual problems. But Jesus did not exclude the
doubter from the apostolate. Nor did He blame him for
having inherited a melancholic disposition. The Lord did
not chide him for desiring satisfying evidence on which to
base his faith, for He knew it was not the unbelief of the
atheist or agnostic, but the doubt of a soul in travail. Archbishop William Temple suggests: "Such vigour of disbelief
plainly represents a strong urge to believe, held down by
common sense and its habitual dread of disillusionment."[4]

The intellectual climate of our day has exalted the question mark into the category of an absolute virtue. Belief
tends to be crucified and unbelief canonized. "I doubt" is
the popular thing to say; not "I believe." But this attitude
finds no support in the teaching of Christ. Doubt is no sign
of superiority. Christ puts no premium on mental dishon-
esty, nor does He suggest that there is any virtue in doubt.
The beatitude is for those who believe, not for those who
doubt.

There is a world of difference between "an evil heart of
unbelief" (Hebrews 3:12, KJV) and the doubts of one who
is weak in faith, between arrogant unbelief and the sensitive questioning of an earnest but hesitant heart. The
doubting of the latter is a regrettable infirmity, but that of
the former is an affront to God.

When unbelieving cavilers demanded a sign, Jesus
promptly refused. "An evil and adulterous generation
craves for a sign; and yet no sign shall be given to it but
the sign of Jonah the prophet" (Matthew 12:39). But when
Thomas wanted not only to hear, but also to see and feel,
Jesus graciously met him in his infirmity.

The beatitude Jesus pronounced on sightless faith was
not an exaltation of credulity or gullibility. He did not endorse a belief without inquiry and consideration, but He

4. William Temple, *Readings in St. John's Gospel,* 2d series: chaps. 13-
21 (London: Macmillan, 1940), p. 390.

did indicate the necessity of a leap of faith. If it be asked what Jesus meant by believing without seeing, the answer probably is: to be satisfied with something less than absolute demonstration. In other words, it means being willing to take the final leap of faith in the risen and living Christ.

It remains to be said that, as in the case of Thomas, God overrules doubt for good. It was Thomas's unbelief that called forth from the Lord the ninth beatitude. When one who doubts does come to faith, he believes the more firmly what he once doubted.

There is a strong tradition that Thomas carried the gospel to Persia, China, and India. The author has had the privilege of ministering to Christians who claim that their church was founded by Thomas, the rapturous confessor.

15

Martha and Mary

Temper or Temperament?

"Mary . . . was listening to the Lord's word, seated at His feet. . . . Martha was distracted with all her preparations" (Luke 10:39-40).

Has not the story of Martha and Mary a special message for us? While the Christian is not to be like the lilies of the field that "toil not, neither do they spin," it is essential for him to remember that where there is work there must also be worship. Both are complimentary—the one must not crowd out the other.[1]

(Reginald G. Russell)

Martha and Mary are so intimately linked in the gospel record that it is difficult to think of one apart from the other. They appear together in three graphic and moving scenes. Martha dominates the first, as hostess in her own home. In the second they are fused together in their grief. In the last, Mary's ardent act of devotion shines like a brilliant star.

A man was once asked which character he preferred, Martha or Mary. With a twinkle in his eye he replied, "I like

1. Reginald G. Russell, "Martha and Mary, Their Message for Today," *The Life of Faith,* May 27, 1942, p. 197.

Martha best before dinner, and Mary best after dinner."
There was more than a grain of truth and wisdom in his
facetious remark, for if you wanted a good dinner, most
likely it would not be Mary's table you would choose. Her
paramount interests lay elsewhere than in the kitchen.

The home at Bethany belonged to Martha (Luke 10:38),
which might indicate that she was a widow. With her lived
Mary, her unmarried sister, and Lazarus, her bachelor
brother. That the family was in comfortable if not affluent
circumstances is reflected in its social eminence, for many
Jews came "to console them concerning their brother"
(John 11:19). Then again, the alabaster vial of very costly
perfume that Mary brought to anoint Jesus with would
give the same impression.

Martha, with her brother and sister, placed their lovely
home at their Master's disposal. It proved to be for Him an
oasis in the arid desert of sin and hostility that he was
increasingly experiencing. Although He was the Son of
God, He was also the Son of Man; and He was most appre-
ciative of the hospitality and kindness of His friends. With
what delight He would come to their home and relax in the
warmth of their companionship, for "Jesus loved Martha,
and her sister, and Lazarus" (John 11:5).

While the Lord's presence in their home brought them
much pleasure and enrichment, it also involved them in a
loss of prestige, for they shared His growing unpopularity.
After the raising of Lazarus, his association with Jesus
became a threat to the authorities; so they conspired to kill
him as well as Jesus.

Martha and Mary provide us with a fascinating study of
temperament in religion, for strong individuality is evident
in each of them. Many of the most intractable problems in
church life can be traced to such variations of temperament, especially when they are accompanied by intolerance and a lack of understanding. Each sister reacted differently to the presence of the Lord, for different people
often act differently in the same situation. There are some
who cannot help regulating the lives of other people, and
Martha was one of the regulators.

Martha's Dinner Party

We first meet the sisters at Martha's home. She had prepared a special meal in honor of their beloved Guest, whose disciples were doubtless also invited, for they were with Him both before and afterward. It was obviously a lavish spread that she was providing, for "Martha was distracted with all her preparations" (Luke 10:40). "Distracted" here means literally "not knowing which way to turn," a condition not unknown even to modern hostesses.

But while Martha was bustling about in the kitchen, preparing a variety of delectable dishes, Mary was in the guest room, placidly sitting at Jesus' feet and drinking in the words of heavenly wisdom that fell from His lips. Meanwhile pressure was building up in the kitchen. Suddenly Martha burst into the guest room and exploded: "Lord, do You not care that my sister has left me to do all the serving alone? Then tell her to help me" (Luke 10:40).

With what regret in coming days would Martha look back on her rudeness to the Lord of glory. She would wish she had cut her tongue out before she turned on the One she so dearly loved. But undisciplined temperament expressed itself in unrestrained temper. She was right to expect that the work of the household should be shared by both sisters, and quite probably Mary was inclined to indulge her reflective temperament and tastes to the neglect of the more mundane tasks of the housewife. But those things did not justify Martha in chiding the Lord.

Jesus did not chide Martha for being of a practical rather than a devotional turn of mind. He had made her so. Had He not Himself toiled at a carpenter's bench? Martha's work as hostess was both necessary and appreciated, but she made three mistakes in the way in which she did it. (1) She so far forgot herself as to rebuke the Lord. (2) She interpreted Mary's devotion to Christ as selfish laziness and despised her for her impractical dreaminess. (3) She became so obsessed with preparing an unnecessarily lavish meal for her guests that she neglected fellowship with the One who would have fed her soul.

Cooking or Company?

Jesus would have preferred Martha's company to the sumptuous meal, and He made that clear when He gently chided her. "Martha, you are worried and bothered about so many things; but only a few things are necessary, really only one" (Luke 10:41-42). It is usually thought that Jesus was referring to the single dish that would have provided an adequate meal, and yet left her enough time to join Mary at His feet. A little economy in food and labor would have paid handsome spiritual dividends.

In spite of Martha's petulant protest, Jesus refused to rebuke or redirect Mary to the kitchen. While not undervaluing Martha's labors of love, Jesus made it clear that man does not live by bread alone. Nor did He suggest that Martha should do exactly what Mary had done. But He did commend Mary for choosing her priorities wisely and putting the more important things first—the spiritual before the temporal. He warmly commended her choice: "Mary has chosen the good part, which shall not be taken away from her" (Luke 10:42).

God gave to each sister, as He gives to each of us, the distinctive talents that would best enable her to discharge her responsibility in the Kingdom. There was no need for one to be envious or critical of the other simply because their devotion to Christ found expression in different ways.

A great deal of incompatibility has its spring in a passion to make other people over in our own likeness. If there is to be a harmonious relationship between people of differing temperaments and backgrounds, there will need to be tolerance, generous understanding, and freedom for people to express their own personalities without unvoiced disapproval.

The lessons arising from the incident are clear and important. We could well emulate the diligence and hospitable spirit of Martha, but it should not be at the expense of time spent sitting at the Master's feet. Brother Lawrence learned the ideal balance between devotion and duty in the drudgery of the monastery kitchen, and from his experience emerged the timeless classic, *The Practice of the Presence of God.* Another lesson is that it is possible to be fervent in spirit without being slothful in business.

It is interesting to note that there was one occasion on which the roles of the sisters were reversed, and we find Martha reacting as we would expect Mary to react. On the occasion we have been considering, it was Mary who sought the Lord's company. But when Lazarus died and the two sisters were convulsed with grief, it was Martha who went to meet Jesus while "Mary still sat in the house" (John 11:20).

Talking and Tears

The second incident finds the sisters overwhelmed with unexpected sorrow. The serious illness of Lazarus caused them to turn at once to the Great Physician, fully confident that He would hasten to their side. But the days passed and He did not come, and they had to experience the agony of losing their brother. Jesus' seemingly inexplicable indifference deeply perplexed and grieved them.

When at last He came and Martha went to meet Him, her greeting held a note of reproach: "Lord, if You had been here"—if You had responded to our appeal instead of staying up north—"my brother would not have died" (John 11:21). But her faith was strong, and it was from practical Martha that the first suggestion of a possible resurrection came. Her conversation with Jesus climaxed in her magnificent confession: "Yes, Lord; I have believed that You are the Christ, the Son of God, even He who comes into the world" (John 11:27).

When Jesus came to Mary, she uttered the same grief-laden words as Martha and then melted into wordless tears. Jesus had been able to talk things through with Martha, but Mary was beyond words. How did He deal with her in her sorrow? "Jesus burst into tears" is the force of John 11:35—tears of genuine love and sympathy. With what deep understanding He ministered to their differing needs according to the temperament of each woman. He talked things over with logical Martha. He wept with the more emotional Mary. He is not less understanding of our own particular temperaments.

Simon's Dinner Party

It was Easter week. The long-anticipated "hour" was rapidly approaching. A grateful Simon, a leper whom Jesus had healed, invited Jesus and His disciples to a feast. Poignantly enough, at about the same time as this happy gathering was taking place, the religious leaders were meeting in Caiaphas's home to plot Christ's death (Matthew 26:3-4). Among the invited guests at Simon's were the Bethany trio. It has been suggested that Simon may have been the father of the three. He had been compelled to live apart from them, the theory goes, because of his leprosy; but this is only conjecture. Martha filled her usual role as hostess, but it was Mary who stole the central place in the picture.

While they were reclining at table, Mary saw a unique opportunity to do something for which she had long sought the occasion. It was no unpremeditated act she was about to perform. At an appropriate moment, she produced her most treasured possession—a beautifully cut vial of alabaster filled with twelve ounces of genuine spikenard, an unguent, or anointing oil. Instead of pouring out a few drops of the costly liquid, she broke the beautiful container and poured the whole over Jesus—it was an expression of deep personal love and devotion.

John emphasizes the costliness of the gift. Judas, the treasurer, estimated its value at three hundred denarii, the equivalent of three hundred days' work. The pure nard, which made it so precious, was a rare aromatic shrub that grew high in the inaccessible Himalayas. Anointing was a common practice in the East, but such a costly perfumed oil was reserved for royalty or the rich.

There is a problem in identifying the occasions on which Jesus was anointed, and the best course, perhaps, is to regard the anointing of Luke 7:36-50 as a different, although similar, event. The fact that in two of the other three accounts Mary anoints the Lord's head (Matthew 26:6-12; Mark 14:3-9), whereas in the third she pours the oil over His feet (John 12:1-8), need not be viewed as a contradiction. In Matthew 26:12 and Mark 14:8, Jesus Himself stated that she had anointed His body. The implication is that the oil poured on His head was also poured on His feet—twelve ounces is a lot of oil! Was her action linked in her thinking with Psalm 133:2? "It is like the precious oil upon the head, coming down upon the beard, . . . coming down upon the edge of his robes."

Mary's wiping of Jesus' feet with her hair was an act of deep humility and abasement. Attending to the feet was a slave's work; and according to Oriental custom, a woman never unbound her hair in public. But Mary's love recognized no such social restriction, so she bathed His feet with her tears; and in an abandonment of love, she wiped them with her hair.

The Indignant Disciples

How did the disciples appraise Mary's action? They were indignant and scolded her (Mark 14:4-5). The charge of extravagance and waste was appropriately laid by Judas Iscariot: "Why was this ointment not sold for three hundred denarii, and given to poor people?" (John 12:5). (It had not taken him long to calculate the sum involved.) His suggestion was not prompted by philanthropy, for John added this illuminating comment: "Now he said this, not because he was concerned about the poor, but because he was a thief, and as he had the money box, he used to pilfer what was put into it" (John 12:6). Had the selflessness of Mary's beautiful action so shown up his cupidity that he was stung into protest?

Loveless hearts are always offended and at a loss to understand the extravagance of love. They are at pains to estimate how little will suffice. Cool and calculating love measures out each little drop. Love like Mary's breaks the container and pours out the whole at the feet of the Lord. True, a few drops would have sufficed to satisfy the custom, but had she done only that, her story would never have survived two millenniums or inspired countless thousands down the years to similar costly acts of love. We must guard against measuring everything by purely utilitarian standards. Do we carefully preserve our little hoard, or do we lavishly pour it out on our Master? Will ours be posthumous benevolence, like that of Joseph of Arimathea, or will we break our alabaster vials now?

Judas was right, of course. The ointment might have been sold and the proceeds devoted to the worthy cause of feeding the poor. Think of the good it could have done instead of being wasted in a single emotional outburst! Yet in His beautiful and unparalleled eulogy, Jesus fully justified Mary's action. "They were scolding her. But Jesus said, 'Let her alone; why do you bother her? She has done a good deed to Me. . . . She has done what she could; she has anointed My body beforehand for the burial. And truly I say to you, wherever the gospel is preached in the whole world, that also which this woman has done shall be spoken of in memory of her' " (Mark 14:5-9).

Although Mary's act of pure and self-forgetful devotion had been misunderstood by others and had earned their censure, to Jesus it was a sweet memory in the testing days ahead. And more than that, through succeeding generations, unnumbered thousands of Christians have thanked God that she did not sell the unguent and give the proceeds to the poor.

Of all His followers, it would appear that Mary alone had perceived the deeper and fuller meaning behind the Lord's references to His impending death. Others besides Mary lovingly prepared choice perfumes and spices for the Lord that Easter, but they were too late! When they brought them to the tomb, He was gone!

Mary decided that if she could not be sure of being able to perform the last offices of love for the dead body of her Lord, she would do it while He was still alive. Of course we do not embalm the living, but Jesus interpreted Mary's act of love in that way: "She has anointed My body beforehand for the burial" (Mark 14:8).

Mary expressed her love while Jesus was still alive to taste its comfort. Too often we leave our eulogies and appreciations until it is too late. Beautiful flowers at a funeral are a poor substitute for the outpouring of love expressed during the lifetime.

16

Barnabas

Mistaken for a God

"*They began calling Barnabas, Zeus [Jupiter]*" (Acts 14:12).

    Certain Bible personalities are very dramatic in their unannouncedness. They appear without any introduction. They burst upon us. . . . Barnabas beams unexpectedly upon the Church like a flood of sunlight. And he was an incarnation of sunshine.[1]

(Dinsdale T. Young)

In the above words, Dinsdale T. Young, that master of the felicitous phrase, introduces one of the most winsome of Bible characters. At first glance Barnabas seems to have been a simple and uncomplicated man. But measured by his character and achievements, he proves to be of unusual stature, and his unspectacular ministry proves to be strangely far-reaching in its influence.

We discover in him an unusual blending of qualities: he is shrewd, yet somewhat unsophisticated; unsuspicious, yet not unduly credulous; gracious and gentle, yet surpris-

---

1. Dinsdale T. Young, *Neglected People of the Bible*, 2d ed. (London: Hodder and Stoughton, 1902), pp. 201-2.

ingly inflexible on occasion; irenic in disposition, yet sufficiently independent to take the lead in what proved to be a revolutionary movement; and above all, "a man with a nature like ours" (James 5:17), subject to the same failures and weaknesses. Such a man has much to teach us.

Not many men have been mistaken for a god! Yet that was Barnabas's experience with the Lycaonians. "They began calling Barnabas, Zeus, and Paul, Hermes, because he was the chief speaker" (Acts 14:12). Zeus was the Greek counterpart of the Roman god Jupiter, and in both mythologies he was the supreme god in their pantheon. They regarded him as the god of power; he controlled the forces of nature.

As the spellbound crowds had heard Paul's flaming preaching, had seen him heal a lifelong cripple, they sensed the presence of the supernatural. "The gods have become like men and have come down to us" was their explanation (Acts 14:11). Apparently his impressive mental stature and commanding personality made a striking impression on them.

A Change of Name

Again, it is not every man who has his name changed so significantly by his friends. But that is what the apostles did with Barnabas. "And Joseph . . . was also called Barnabas by the apostles (which translated means, Son of Encouragement)" (Acts 4:36). His genius was of the heart rather than of the head, but it was nonetheless genius.

The change of name was eloquent of the gracious ministry Barnabas exercised thus early in his Christian life. The name has been translated variously: "son of consolation," "son of comfort," "son of exhortation"—an attractive nickname, and one to be coveted. The name mirrored the ministry. Barnabas had the gift of prophecy. "One who prophesies speaks to men for edification and exhortation and consolation" (1 Cor. 14:3). Paul was "chief speaker," but to his weighty utterances Barnabas added his fervent exhortations.

This ministry of consolation and encouragement is not

to be regarded as inferior and of secondary importance. Did it not characterize our Lord, of whom it was prophesied, "A bruised reed He will not break, and a dimly burning wick He will not extinguish" (Isaiah 42:3)? In his closing years Dr. F. B. Meyer said that if he had his life to live over again, he would devote much more time to the ministry of comfort and encouragement. Did we but discern it, we are daily surrounded by lonely, aching, and sometimes broken hearts. Did not this ability of Barnabas to impart comfort to others stem from the fact that he was full of the Comforter?

Luke tells us that Barnabas was "a Levite of Cyprian birth" (Acts 4:36). As Cyprus and Cilicia, of which Tarsus was the capital, formed a single Roman province, there was a sense in which Saul and Barnabas were fellow citizens. As Barnabas came from an affluent family, it is quite possible that he had been sent to Tarsus for his education, and there he may have met Saul. Tradition affirms that he, like Saul, had been taught by the famous Gamaliel.

His racial background would find him acceptance in Antioch, for it was from men of Cyprus and Cyrene that people at Antioch had first heard the gospel (Acts 11:20). As a Levite, too, he would be well versed in the Scriptures of the Old Testament. A Levite's becoming a follower of Christ involved a renunciation that often resulted in ostracism by friends and family.

Consecrated Stewardship

An act of spontaneous generosity first brought Barnabas to prominence in the infant church; it was an action that stirred an unholy emulation in the heart of Ananias. Barnabas, "who owned a tract of land, sold it and brought the money and laid it at the apostles' feet" (Acts 4:37). That act of Christian generosity gives insight into the character of this delightful man. He viewed his ownership as a stewardship.

The very brevity of the record could conceal the significance and costliness of the act. In the land-hungry East, where ownership of the smallest piece of land is a jealously guarded privilege from generation to generation, the sacrifice involved was very great. Barnabas was surrendering his financial independence. Originally, Levites were not permitted to own property, but the passing of the years had resulted in the ignoring of this prohibition. So, like his Master, though he was rich he became poor. How many similar sacrifices have been inspired by Barnabas's unselfish example?

There is a pleasing touch in the fact that the man who had given away his own money had the joy of distributing the generosity of others to those in need (Acts 11:30).

In nature Barnabas was *unsuspicious but not unduly credulous.* His charitable and optimistic temperament readily enabled him to put the best construction on ambiguous conduct, but he nevertheless had a keen insight into character. Men of this type often see more clearly than those with suspicious eyes. Not only was he unsuspicious himself, but he was able to dispel suspicion from the minds of those whose confidence he won.

A Daring Selection

Perhaps Barnabas saw in the former persecutor the potential church leader. Barnabas's discernment was confirmed as God worked mightily in Paul's life. When Saul came to Jerusalem, "he was trying to associate with the disciples; and they were all afraid of him, not believing that he was a disciple. *But Barnabas* took hold of him and brought him to the apostles" (Acts 9:26-27, italics added). While the other Christians were scenting a clever ruse, large-hearted Barnabas sponsored Saul to the apostles. He was the lonely Saul's first Christian friend. Thus Barnabas opened the door for him to become the apostle to the Gentiles.

His *magnanimity of spirit* is further seen in his seeking Saul as his colleague in the rapidly spreading revival at Antioch. Apparently it required diligent search to locate him (Acts 11:25); so, for a second time, Barnabas saw in Paul one who could serve the church.

The warm fellowship of the Antioch Christians drew

increasing crowds, and Barnabas recognized that the work was beyond his unaided efforts. With divinely imparted insight, he chose as his colleague the former Jewish zealot. It was a stroke of genius, a daring choice that proved to be "one of the most successful experiments in the history of the church." So Barnabas was the instrument in bringing together the world's greatest missionary and what became the model missionary church.

Only a big man would have made such a selection, for to a man of Barnabas's discernment it would be obvious that this dynamic and brilliant scholar would speedily outshine and outstrip him. He was *willing to accept a subordinate role*, in the interests of the Kingdom. He did not feel that it demeaned him to give place to a less experienced but more able junior. Unostentatiously he slipped into second place with not the slightest evidence of jealousy.

It would be difficult to exaggerate the influence on Paul of his early association with Barnabas. Paul's socially exclusive background and training tended to make him bigoted and narrow, but those tendencies were mellowed and redirected through the training of his generous mentor.

Barnabas Fans the Revival

Barnabas displayed *rare tact* in the sensitive situation he faced at Antioch. When the revival movement in Gentile Antioch began to gather momentum, the Jerusalem leaders became apprehensive about the direction it might take. They were reluctant to imperil their own orthodoxy by identifying with the unpredictable movement, but they wisely decided to send Barnabas as their delegate and observer (Acts 11:22).

"They sent down men to regularize what they could not produce," said E. Stanley Jones. "The lay group produced the spiritual movements, and the apostles tried to regularize them."[2]

We can see the divine overruling in their choice of Bar-

2. E. Stanley Jones, *Mastery* (London: Hodder and Stoughton, 1946), p. 131.

nabas. Had their delegate been a hard-line legalist, the story might well have been different. With open arms, Barnabas welcomed the new believers into the wider fellowship of the church. The whole missionary movement owes much to Barnabas, and no better envoy could have been sent to cement relationships and encourage the developing church.

His outlook on life was characterized by *a healthy optimism*. He hoped all things and expected the best of people—and usually got it. Was not this behind his championing of Mark in spite of Paul's opposition? And could he not claim in the end that his optimism was justified? No wonder they called him a son of encouragement. No one is encouraged by pessimism.

Added to these desirable qualities of character was no small degree of *physical courage* in the face of persecution and danger. "Our beloved Barnabas and Paul, men who have risked their lives for the name of our Lord Jesus Christ" (Acts 15:25-26). This was the testimony of the church at Jerusalem to its intrepid brethren.

But the highest tribute comes from Luke: "He [Barnabas] was a good man, and full of the Holy Spirit and of faith" (Acts 11:24). In our sophisticated society, goodness is a neglected waif. Although it stands high in God's category of virtues, it is accorded scant courtesy. But goodness, which can be defined as "active benevolence," was characteristic of Barnabas's Lord, who "went about doing good" (Acts 10:38). Barnabas was a good man whose normal experience was to be full of the Holy Spirit, completely under His control. Because he was also "full . . . of faith," he appropriated the divine resources made available by the Holy Spirit.

Not Exempt from Failure

Being a good man and full of the Holy Spirit does not preclude the possibility of failure. This attractive man was not a perfect man. The treasure was there, but in an earthen vessel. His strong point proved to be his weak point, and on two occasions Barnabas disappointed his colleague Paul.

In their missionary work among the Gentiles, these two men were united in their purpose to ignore the legalistic outlook of the Jerusalem hierarchy and to identify with the Gentile believers at Antioch. The sad sequel is recorded by Paul: "Prior to the coming of certain men from James, he [Peter] used to eat with the Gentiles; but when they came, he began to withdraw and hold himself aloof, fearing the party of the circumcision. And the rest of the Jews joined him in hypocrisy, with the result that even Barnabas was carried away by their hypocrisy" (Galatians 2:12-13).

"Even Barnabas": that was a heartrending blow to Paul. It was bad enough that Peter should yield to the pressure group from Jerusalem, but that his own beloved colleague and senior missionary who had stood loyally with him in Jerusalem should join in the defection was the unkindest cut of all.

It might not have been so serious had Peter's and his followers' action been the expression of sincere conviction. But Paul's charge is that "they were not straightforward about the truth of the gospel" (Galations 2:14). They acted hypocritically, not sincerely. The major blame is laid at Peter's door, but the fact that Barnabas was swept along in the hypocrisy laid bare one of the weaknesses in his attractive personality. Virtue easily degenerates into vice, and Barnabas's genial magnanimity led to a lack of steadfastness in the face of unpopularity.

The seriousness of his failure lies in the fact that not only did he embarrass and desert his friend and colleague, but he insulted the believers at Antioch. And worse still, he imperiled their Christian liberty and perhaps that of the whole church.

By special revelation, God had shown Peter that the Gentiles held an equal status with the Jews in Christ's church, but for the sake of keeping the favor of the narrow sectarians at Jerusalem, he had been disobedient to the heavenly vision and had dragged Barnabas down with

him. If Paul had shrunk from opposing Peter to his face
(Galations 2:11), the whole Christian movement might
have foundered. The lesson of this incident for us is that
even our strong points need constant watchfulness, lest
they degenerate into weakness.

Beneficiaries of the Second Chance

It might be argued that the foregoing incident paved the
way for the more serious quarrel that developed between
Barnabas and Paul. On the first missionary journey, John
Mark, a nephew of Barnabas, had defected at Perga and
returned home. Paul regarded that as a serious dereliction
of duty. Later, when Barnabas of the tender heart desired
to take Mark with them on their return visit, Paul objected. He maintained that Mark lacked the stamina and
strength of purpose necessary for so hazardous an adventure and that his presence would be a hindrance rather
than a help.

From Luke's account of the incident, it seems clear that
this was no mild spat, but a serious quarrel. "There arose
such a sharp disagreement," says Luke, "that they sepa-
rated from one another, and Barnabas took Mark with him
and sailed away to Cyprus. But Paul chose Silas and departed, being committed by the brethren to the grace of
the Lord" (Acts 15:39-40).

There is no doubt that Barnabas's action smacked of
nepotism, but it may also have been prompted by the con-
victions that the young man should be given a second
chance and that he would ultimately make good. How
many of us have been beneficiaries of the second chance!
Barnabas was caught in a clash of loyalties, and he opted
in favor of his nephew.

In the heat of the argument, the mildness of Barnabas
became obstinacy, and Paul's firmness became intransi-
gence. As neither would give way, the only solution to the
impasse was for each to go his separate way. There is no
record of their praying over the problem. But was this the
best solution, or the only one? In retrospect it can be seen
that there were elements of truth in both viewpoints. It

would seem, as Ramsay suggests, that history marches with Paul in the dispute, for he and not Barnabas received the blessing of the church at Antioch.

On the other hand, Barnabas's conviction of the salvability of Mark was also vindicated by subsequent events. The salutary lesson of the quarrel may have opened Mark's eyes to his own character defect and caused him to seek and obtain divine help to overcome it.

The quarrel cannot be justified or condoned, but God has a gracious way of turning the curse into a blessing. The young man made good. No bitterness remained between the two friends, for Paul said to Timothy, "Pick up Mark and bring him with you, for he is useful to me for service" (2 Timothy 4:11). Paul was big enough to concede that the optimistic forecast of Barnabas had been vindicated and that his own fears had been unwarranted. In the providence of God, out of the regrettable crisis there emerged two experienced missionary teams instead of one to spearhead the advance into heathendom.

Similar tragic but unnecessary quarrels have been enacted on many mission fields. Good and strong people, deeply committed to the work of God, argue their own divergent points of view but do not pray through. That makes them an open target for the enemy. The wrong in this case lay not in the argument itself, but in the spirit in which it was conducted. The word Luke uses to describe it is the equivalent of our *paroxysm*, and it is no fruit of the Spirit. When Paul used the same word when he wrote that love "is not provoked" (1 Corinthians 13:5), did he have his own failure in mind?

A fifth-century manuscript entitled *The Acts of Barnabas* records Barnabas's martydrom and burial at Salamis, his home town—a worthy end to a worthy life.

"Lovely and pleasant as was Barnabas, what is he to his Lord and Master? . . . The glory of Barnabas is stellar glory, the glory of Christ is solar splendour."[3]

3. Young, p. 223.

17

Stephen

The Man of Five Fullnesses

*"Select . . . men . . . full of . . . wisdom. . . . They chose
Stephen, a man full of faith and of the Holy Spirit. . . .
Stephen, full of grace and power"* (Acts 6:3, 5, 8).

Stephen, strong-minded, aware of a wider world and supremely intelligent, had grasped the vital fact that what had
happened in Palestine was a climax and a consummation of
a vast sweep of history, which began with the call of Abraham. . . . He traces an unfolding purpose of God, but subtly
stresses the spiritual ancestry of the group he had before
him, ready to resist the Lord who sought to save them, and
prompt to persecute even Moses who set out to deliver them.[1]

(E. M. Blaiklock)

Stephen does not usually figure among the major personalities of Scripture, yet he occupies a unique niche in
the history of the Christian church. Altogether apart from
his noble qualities of character, in the providence of God
he burst into Hebrew history at an extremely critical moment.

1. E. M. Blaiklock et al., *Bible Characters and Doctrines*, 16 vols.
(Grand Rapids: Eerdmans, 1972-75), vol. 13, *Ananias to Paul/The
Kingdom and the Church* (1975), p. 35.

It is no exaggeration to say that Stephen's marytrdom was a pivotal and epoch-making moment in the ongoing purpose of God. Luke presents it as the fulcrum on which the future of world evangelization was poised. Everything in the first half of the book of Acts leads up to it or stems from it. The whole story is concerned with God's global missionary plan. Of no one has it proved more true that the blood of the martyrs is the seed of the church. Stephen's name comes from the Greek word for a crown, strangely prophetic of the martyr's crown he was to wear.

A Determining Crisis

The following Scriptures indicate the nature of the determining crisis of Stephen's martyrdom:

> On that day a great persecution arose against the church in Jerusalem; and they were all scattered throughout the regions of Judea and Samaria [cf. Acts 1:8], except the apostles. . . . *Therefore*, those who had been scattered went about preaching the word (Acts 8:1, 4, italics added). So then those who were scattered because of the persecution that arose in connection with Stephen made their way to Phoenicia and Cyprus and Antioch, speaking the word *to no one except to Jews alone.* But there were some of them, men of Cyprus and Cyrene, who came to Antioch and *began speaking to the Greeks also,* preaching the Lord Jesus. . . . And a large number who believed turned to the Lord (Acts 11:19-21, italics added).

The reluctant and exclusive Christians in Jerusalem had not been impelled by the love of Christ to take His gospel outside their own nation. The genius of the Great Commission had not gripped them, nor had their Lord's worldwide vision become theirs. Even when the great persecution broke on them and they had to flee, their witness was to "no one except to Jews alone."

So fierce was their racialism that even the fires of persecution did not melt it. But under the influence of the Spirit, some broke through the racial barrier "and began speaking to the Greeks also." One result was the church at Antioch, the church whose missionary zeal set the world aflame. Stephen's martyrdom was thus a watershed from which the river of life was deflected into the Gentile world.

Some scholars believe that a second factor that lent great significance to Stephen's martyrdom was the influence it exerted on Paul, the apostle to the Gentiles. Without doubt, next to its Founder, Paul was the most influential character in the universal church (Acts 7:58; 8:1). This event played a major part in Paul's conversion, they say; and it is in large measure to his conversion that we owe the gospel liberty we enjoy today. But for his strong championing of the believer's liberty in Christ, Christianity might easily have degenerated into another exclusive Jewish sect.

Stephen's courage, faith, and invincible love might have weakened Paul's resistance to the gospel. "When the blood of Thy witness Stephen was being shed," he recalled, "I also was standing by approving, and watching out for the cloaks of those who were slaying him" (Acts 22:20). Augustine declared that had Stephen not prayed, the church would not have had Paul.[2]

Spiritual Maturity

The martyr's powerful witness and the influence of his life should be viewed in the light of the fact that he was not a mature Christian with years of experience behind him. He had been a Christian for not more than four years. Spiritual maturity is not a matter of gray hairs, nor does it develop automatically with the passing of the years. Young Christians who have abandoned their lives without reservation to the Lordship of Christ and are filled with the Spirit often display greater maturity in their reactions to the testing circumstances of life than many who have long been Christians.

Again, Stephen was not an apostle, but a layman who

2. In William G. Moorehead, *Outline Studies in Acts, Romans, First and Second Corinthians, Galatians and Ephesians* (New York: Revell, 1902), p. 17.

had risen from the ranks. Faithfulness in the exercise of his gifts in a humbler position won for him a more privileged ministry and high honor in the Kingdom of God. His genuine piety and gifts of nature and grace elevated him to costly leadership in the church.

Like Philip, Stephen owed his appointment as one of the first deacons of the Jerusalem church to a social problem that was having harmful side effects. The problem was not surprising, for it would be surprising if the devil allowed the success of the church to go unchallenged. Disaffection had developed among the Greek-speaking Jews, who alleged that their widows were being discriminated against in the distribution of food and relief.

The apostles recognized the potential seriousness of the rift that had occurred, and they urged the church to select seven men "of good reputation, full of the Spirit and of wisdom" (Acts 6:3) to oversee this administrative task. The apostles would continue to devote themselves to their primary responsibilities of prayer and the ministry of the Word. Stephen was the first-named of the selected men, and he was doubtless first in importance too (Acts 6:5).

A Life of Copious Overflow

Stephen's life was one of copious overflow. Five times over, fullness is predicated of him. Three times he is said to be *full of the Holy Spirit* (Acts 6:3, 5; 7:55). The other four fullnesses flowed from this inexhaustible reservoir.

The basic idea of the word "full" in these passages is that of mastery and control. Not *something* poured into him, but *Someone* taking possession and control of him at his invitation and with his full consent. The Spirit-filled man is simply one whose whole personality is interpenetrated and controlled by the Holy Spirit. This enabled the Holy Spirit, no longer grieved or quenched, to manifest His power in Stephen's life to such a marked degree.

He was *full of wisdom* (Acts 6:3, 10). He possessed that sensitive insight that enables a man to see right to the heart of things. It is knowledge, but it is more than knowledge. It is the faculty of putting our knowledgde to the best possible use. In the delicate situation that had arisen in the church, wisdom was a quality greatly needed. The Spirit gave Stephen an ability in debate so incisive that he routed opponents from three continents. "They were unable to cope with the wisdom and the Spirit with which he was speaking" (Acts 6:10). The Spirit of God places no premium on ignorance, but He makes full use of knowledge carefully acquired.

Stephen was *full of grace* (Acts 6:8). Grace is one of the richest words in the Bible; it is a word that has far outgrown its humble beginnings. It is undeserved love that passes far beyond the claims of love. It is the spirit that deals with unworthy people not according to their deserts, but according to the yearning of its own heart. It is the antithesis of the censorious and judgmental attitude of mind, for grace produces graciousness, a flower that bloomed in profusion in Stephen's heart.

He was *full of faith* (Acts 6:5). His was a believing, trustful, expectant frame of mind. He was a chronic believer, just as Thomas was a chronic doubter. What God had spoken, he believed without question or reservation. His strong faith made him a great receiver of God's gifts. Because Stephen had such unlimited confidence in the faithfulness of God, God was able to entrust him with unlimited spiritual power.

He was *full of power* (Acts 6:8). His was not the power of rhetoric or of intellect alone, although he possessed those powers in full measure. Nor was it the power of a magnetic personality, which he undoubtedly possessed. It was the power of the Holy Spirit's personality working through him that enabled him so effectively to proclaim the gospel, defend the faith, and endure a martyr's death. His testimony won the favor of the people, but it stirred up the virulent hatred of the synagogue.

Inevitably Stephen was drawn into debate with the Jews who had come from several lands. Unable to refute his arguments, they resorted to bribing false witnesses. "They secretly induced men to say, 'We have heard him speak blasphemous words against Moses and against God.' And they stirred up the people, the elders and the scribes, and they came upon him and dragged him away, and brought him before the Council. And they put forward false witnesses who said, 'This man incessantly speaks against this holy place, and the Law; for we have heard him say that this Nazarene, Jesus, will destroy this place'" (Acts 6:11-14). As the priests depended on the Temple for their livelihood, they could not ignore such a charge.

But as the members of the Council glared at him, all the members of the Sanhedrin saw his face radiating with celestial glory, "like the face of an angel" (Acts 6:15).

On being challenged by the high priest, Stephen embarked on his apology, for his speech took the form of an apologia for the gospel rather than a defense of himself. An apology is a statement made in vindication of one's position rather than of one's person. Stephen's speech, which occupies most of Acts 7, is the longest sermon in the book. Remarkably, Stephen delivered the whole of his address without mentioning the name of Jesus once! The Lord is, however, indirectly referred to in Acts 7:52, but He is, of course, the focus of the whole discourse.

An Eloquent Apology

In his remarkable and eloquent sermon, Stephen revealed his accurate grasp of Jewish history and its relevance to the new faith he had embraced. He turned the tables on his attackers and charged them with being the guilty ones. He refuted their charges in a closely reasoned, eloquent speech that reviewed their history from the time of Abraham onward. From it he demonstrated that the presence of the eternal God cannot be localized and confined to an earthly temple, be it ever so magnificent.

He cited God's presence with Joseph even when he was in Egypt. He reminded them that as a nation they had persistently rejected and resisted the messengers of God. They had envied and mistreated Joseph, whom God had sent as their preserver. They had rebelled against Moses and rejected his message. They had stoned the prophets and abused the functions of the Temple. They boasted of the angelic mediation of the Law, yet they failed to keep it.

Stephen then demonstrated that the Jesus they had so recently murdered was the Righteous One, the Prophet whose coming Moses prophesied, and the One whom they should have received instead of murdering (Acts 7:35, 52). He summed up his charge against them in the accusing words: "You are doing just as your fathers did" (Acts 7:51).

The apology revealed Stephen's amazing insight into the purpose and spiritual significance of God's dealings with Israel and showed the relevance of Jesus in religious history. It was *the first inspired commentary* on the Old Testament by a New Testament Christian.

Alleged Discrepancies

It is sometimes alleged that in Stephen's historical review there are two discrepancies. In Acts 7:6, Israel's bondage in Egypt is stated as 400 years; whereas in Exodus 12:40 the figure is 430 years. It is interesting that Josephus mentions both figures, while Philo gives 400.[3] It is quite possible that both figures are correct, but are reckoned from different starting points. It may be that 430 is the exact figure, but that Stephen gave a round figure, as we sometimes do.

The other problem arises over Acts 7:14, in which the descendants of Jacob are said to be seventy-five; whereas Genesis 46:27 says seventy. In the Greek Septuagint version from which, as a Hellenist, Stephen would quote, the number is made up to seventy-five by adding to the list of Genesis 46:8-27 the names of Manasseh's son Machir and grandson Gilead, and Ephraim's sons Shuthelah and Taam and his grandson Edom.

When Stephen delivered his final, blistering denunciation, he did it with his eyes open. He knew what the inevitable reaction of those bigoted men would be when he told them that they were stiff-necked, uncircumcised in heart, and murderers and betrayers of the Righteous One (Acts 7:51-52).

---

3. In Thomas Walker, *The Acts of the Apostles* (Chicago: Moody, 1965), p. 156.

Cut to the heart by charges they could not refute, the religious leaders cut short Stephen's defense and gnashed their teeth at him in insensate rage. The whole proceedings were entirely illegal and irregular, as they had been with Jesus. Like Him, Stephen was falsely accused; no formal charge was laid, no evidence called or considered, no vote taken, no verdict announced, no sentence passed. They took the law into their own hands, even though Rome had deprived them of the right to administer capital punishment.

The Heavenly Vision

God never deserts His witnesses in their hour of need. To Stephen He granted the glorious vision that sustained him through the hail of stones that rained on him. Gazing intently into heaven, he "saw the glory of God, and Jesus standing at the right hand of God" (Acts 7:55). He may never have seen Jesus in the flesh, but instinctively he recognized Him as the Son of Man (Acts 7:56) in the place of honor and majesty, standing as though to welcome His persecuted servant.

When he cried, "Behold, I see the heavens opened up and the Son of Man" (Acts 7:56), it was too much for the infuriated mob. They stopped their ears so as not to listen to any more such blasphemy, rushed on him, dragged him out of the city through what is now known as St. Stephen's Gate, and began stoning him. Like his Master, he had to suffer outside the gate. Like Him, too, Stephen died praying.

As the stones kept raining on his battered body, reeling under their attack, he knelt and with upturned and radiant face called on the Lord and said, "Lord Jesus, receive my spirit" (Acts 7:59). His last breath carried a prayer for his murderers, poignantly reminiscent of our Lord's words from the cross. "Lord, do not hold this sin against them," he prayed (Acts 7:60; cf. Luke 23:34). Having uttered the prayer, he laid his head on Jesus' breast and "fell asleep" (Acts 7:60).

Devout friends took Stephen's tortured body and gave him an honorable burial with great lamentation. Moved though they were at the loss of their friend and perhaps fearful for what might lie ahead of them, they did not realize that they had witnessed one of the great crises of church history. But the scene that caused great grief to the Christians only aroused Saul and his friends to a greater frenzy. "On that day a great persecution arose against the church in Jerusalem" (Acts 8:1).

Stephen was only the first of that noble army of men and women who have been faithful unto death and have won the martyr's crown. What has his martyrdom to teach us? What power enabled him to witness so fearlessly and suffer so triumphantly? The days of martyrs are not past, for as this is being written, news has just come of two friends who have earned the martyr's crown.

The overriding factor in Stephen's life was that being full of the Spirit was his normal condition. He had an uninterrupted vision of the exalted Christ (Acts 7:55). He cherished a hope unquenched by persecution (Acts 7:59). No bitterness was harbored in his heart; instead, he prayed for his enemies (Acts 7:60).

To Stephen, death was only sleep—not a terminus, only a junction.

18

Philip

Deacon, Revivalist, Missionary

"Philip . . . began proclaiming Christ to them. . . . Philip . . . preached Jesus to him" (Acts 8:5, 35).

When he [Philip] was chosen with the other six to look after the temporal, material interests and wellbeing of certain members of the church, we are not to think that this was an unspiritual task. Here was an area that was just as spiritual as was the preaching of the Word by Peter or Paul. I wish I could say something to encourage our lay people to believe that serving in capacities in the church in which they have to handle money, or deal with administrative problems . . . when it is done unto the Saviour in the power of His spirit, is as spiritual as preaching a sermon or leading a prayer.[1]

(Paul S. Rees)

First a deacon, then a revivalist, then a missionary; privileged to win for Christ the first Gentile convert of foreign missions, who in turn became the pioneer of the gospel to a nation and a continent. This, in a nutshell, is the biography of Philip the evangelist.

---

1. Paul S. Rees, *Men of Action in the Book of Acts* (Westwood, N.J.: Revell, n.d.), p. 61.

He appears first on the pages of Scripture as one of the seven deacons of the infant church at Jerusalem. They owed their appointment to the social problem that had arisen in the Christian community, a problem to which reference was made in the last chapter. The non-Palestinian Jews were complaining that in the daily distribution of food, there was discrimination against their needy widows by the native Hebrews (Acts 6:1). While recognizing the validity of the charge, the twelve apostles discerned in the crisis an attempt of Satan to deflect them from their primary responsibilities—an ever present temptation to the Christian worker.

The apostles shared their conviction with the congregation: "It is not desirable for us to neglect the word of God in order to serve table. But select from among you, brethren, seven men of good reputation, full of the Spirit and of wisdom, whom we may put in charge of this task. But we will devote ourselves to prayer, and to the ministry of the word" (Acts 6:2-4). This inspired and inspiring leadership held momentous implications for the new movement.

Second in the list of those selected to engage in this social work was Philip, a Greek-speaking Jew. He, with the other six, was responsible for the temporal and economic welfare of the widows of the church. The qualifications the apostles demanded for this seemingly routine administrative task seem more appropriate for those whose ministry was praying and preaching. But thus early in the life of the church the Holy Spirit impressed on the believers that even for temporal responsibilities, more than secular qualifications were necessary. The appointees had to be men of integrity, "of good reputation"; spirituality, "full of the Spirit"; and sagacity, "full . . . of wisdom" (Acts 6:3). " 'Secular men' have absolutely no place in the administration of the affairs of the church of Christ, all of which are 'sacred' to the Holy Spirit."[2]

The wisdom and overruling of the Spirit are seen in the subsequent careers of some of the men selected for this

2. Arthur T. Pierson, *The Acts of the Holy Spirit* (New York: Revell, 1895), p. 62.

task. The apostles chose deacons to perform a common function, but God gave them martyrs and evangelists, mighty men of God.

A minor task faithfully discharged is often only preliminary to a larger call, and that was the case with Philip. The Lord had specified the spheres of witness of His disciples (Acts 1:8), but the Jerusalem church had failed to rise to the Lord's commission. It had gone beyond its own borders only when the great persecution struck it. Then "they that were scattered abroad went every where preaching the word" (Acts 8:4, KJV). But even then, so strong was their racial prejudice that they were "speaking the word to no one except to Jews alone" (Acts 11:19).

A Witness to Samaria

Philip was one of the Jews of the Dispersion, but he burst through the racial barriers, and we next find him proclaiming Christ in Samaria. This was a radical departure, for "Jews have no dealings with Samaritans" (John 4:9). The reason for this antipathy lay in the fact that the Samaritans were a hybrid race, descended from Jews who were left in northern Palestine and the heathen with whom they intermarried. They had their own version of the Pentateuch; they retained a mixture of Mosaic ritual and teaching, but diluted it with heathen practices. The fact that they entertained a strong Messianic hope gave Philip a fine starting point for his gospel.

To orthodox Jews the Samaritans were traitors, worse than pure pagans and utterly to be shunned. The Jew who opened the door of the Kingdom to the Samaritans was the Lord Himself (John 4:7-42). Philip followed in his Master's footsteps and was the first to fulfill the wider reaches of the Great Commission. His position as the pioneer evangelist and missionary has not been adequately appreciated. As Philip moved about in the semipagan city, the fire burned in his heart as he shared the gospel with the people. The Spirit's blessing rested upon his preaching and confirmed his witness by enabling him to exorcise demons and perform miracles of healing.

The Samaritan Revival

Philip was soon in the midst of a great revival movement. "The multitudes with one accord were giving attention to what was said by Philip, as they heard and saw the
signs which he was performing" (Acts 8:6). The movement
was on such a large scale that the apostles in Jerusalem
felt it necessary to send Peter and John as a special deputation to investigate and to share the blessings flowing
from Pentecost (Acts 8:14-17). When they arrived, they
found the city effervescent with joy (Acts 8:8). It is of more
than passing interest that the John who desired Jesus to
call down fire on the Samaritans and consume them was
the one now chosen to impart the fire of the Holy Spirit to
them. What a vast transformation Pentecost had made in
him.

Philip's work was no flash in the pan, for we read of the
church in Samaria that it was "being built up; and, going
on in the fear of the Lord and in the comfort of the Holy
Spirit, it continued to increase" (Acts 9:31).

At the time of Philip's arrival, Samaria was under the
spell of a famous sorcerer, well known to subsequent history as Simon Magus. It was through him that the gospel
was first confronted with the pseudospiritual systems that
abounded in the East at that time. They were compounds
of astrology and sorcery, sweetened with a dash of science.
By exploiting the superstitions of the Samaritans, Simon
had attained great influence and stature, so much so that
he was called "the Great Power of God" (Acts 8:10).

He must have been greatly disconcerted when Philip appeared performing miracles of healing and exorcism that
made him look like an amateur (Acts 8:7, 13). Accustomed
as he was to amazing others with his spurious phenomena
and paraphernalia, Simon was now to be amazed.

He could not deny the evidence of his eyes, and Luke
records that "even Simon himself believed" (Acts 8:13).
When other converts sought Christian baptism, Simon
joined them. But as Cyril put it, "he was *baptized*, but he
was not *illuminated*."[3] He became a zealous follower of

3. In Thomas Walker, *The Acts of the Apostles* (Chicago: Moody, 1965),
   p. 190.

Philip, going with him from place to place. It was a notable triumph for the church, but the triumph was to prove shortlived.

Spiritual Gifts Cannot Be Purchased

Under the instruction and prayers of Peter and John, the Samaritans received a share in the Pentecostal Gift (Acts 8:17). When Simon saw the mighty effect of the Spirit's operation, his covetous, carnal heart craved the same power so that he could enhance his own reputation and add another dimension to his magical arts.

Events soon proved that his intellectual assent to the facts of the gospel had not been accompanied by the consent of his will to its spiritual implications, for he offered the apostles money in exchange for the spiritual gift. It was this blasphemous act that has given us our word *simony*, which we use to indicate the sin of seeking spiritual preferment in exchange for money (Acts 8:18). Simon thus betrayed the fact that his real interest lay in the miraculous manifestations he had seen, not in the holiness the Spirit would impart. He wanted to add them to his repertoire.

The Spirit-filled Peter immediately discerned Simon's hypocrisy and scathingly denounced him: "May your silver perish with you, because you thought you could obtain the gift of God with money!" (Acts 8:20). Accompanying his denunciation, there was a plea to repent (Acts 8:21-22).

Simon was terror-stricken that he had incurred the wrath of men who possessed such awesome powers, and he asked for their prayers "so that nothing of what you have said may come upon me" (Acts 8:24). His very plea for prayer revealed the accuracy of Peter's diagnosis when he said, "You have no part or portion in this matter, for your heart is not right before God" (Acts 8:21). Simon's expression of concern did not spring from sorrow for sin, but from fear of punishment. He had been baptized, but he had experienced no change of heart. Through Peter's spiritual discernment, the church successfully repulsed a satanic attack on its purity.

From Multitudes to an Individual

Suddenly, in the midst of these stirring revival scenes, the Lord of the harvest redirected His servant. "An angel of the Lord spoke to Philip saying, 'Arise and go south to the road that descends from Jerusalem to Gaza.' (This is a desert road.)" (Acts 8:26).

Gaza lay to the southwest of Samaria and was an important center of traffic, as the main road passed through it.

It is not always realized that it was by Philip the deacon, not by Peter the apostle, that the wider implementation of the Great Commission began to be fulfilled. To leave a thriving and thrilling work that he had initiated in order to take a journey under sealed orders to a desert area must have been a costly experience for the evangelist. He could think up a dozen reasons why he could not be spared, but his spiritual maturity is seen in his reaction. "He arose and went" (Acts 8:27)—no argument, no delay. He did not know how much hinged upon the promptness of his obedience.

The road he was to take would intersect the road from Jerusalem to Ethiopia at a certain spot. Had he delayed five minutes to argue the reasonableness of the command with the messenger, he would have missed the divinely arranged appointment with the influential Ethiopian prince, and Africa would have been denied the gospel at that stage. The lesson for us needs little elaboration. Our tardiness in obeying the promptings of the Spirit can rob us and others of the blessing God has planned to give.

The Ethiopia of that day included all of Africa south of Egypt. Under Queen Candace it had developed a remarkable civilization. It was customary to employ eunuchs in high positions. The treasurer of Queen Candace's kingdom and a member of her cabinet was a eunuch, and it was he whom Philip accosted when Philip met his chariot.

The eunuch had traveled to Jerusalem to worship—he was an important foreign official with a hungry heart. He had joined in the ritual and worship of the Temple, but the glory had departed. All was cold and dead. He found no balm for his seeking soul. However, he had purchased a roll of the Old Testament, and he beguiled the tedium of his long homeward journey by reading it.

Divine Providence

The timing of Philip's encounter with the Ethiopian eunuch bore all the marks of divine providence. He was reading aloud in Isaiah's prophecy, and as the chariot drew alongside, "the Spirit said to Philip, 'Go up and join this chariot' " (Acts 8:29). The traveler was trying to puzzle out the meaning of what he was reading, but without success. He could make no sense out of Isaiah's words. "Do you understand what you are reading?" Philip asked. "Well, how could I, unless someone guides me" was the wistful response (Acts 8:30-31). Was it by chance that he was reading the chapter in the Old Testament that reveals, more than any other, Christ as the Suffering Servant and Savior? Was it by chance that the one man in the area who could explain the prophet's meaning was sitting next to him?

To the question "Please tell me, of whom does the prophet say this? Of himself, or of someone else?" (Acts 8:34), Philip had a ready answer. Never did a preacher have a more attentive and interested audience than did Philip as he "opened his mouth, and . . . preached Jesus to him" (Acts 8:35). In addition to explaining the inner meaning of the cross of Christ, Philip must have shown the place and importance of Christian baptism, for no sooner had the eunuch embraced Christ than he was asking to be baptized (Acts 8:36). The natural and inevitable result of his obedience was that he "went on his way rejoicing" (Acts 8:39).

The whole incident is a moving illustration of the interest God has in the individual. He goes to endless pains to bring one seeking heart to salvation. To achieve His end, he will take a prominent church leader away from a ministry to multiplied thousands so that he can meet the need of a single enquirer. But what an enquirer! Irenaeus tells us that he became a missionary to his own people.[4]

4. Irenaeus *Against Heresies* 3:12.8.

Philip had now completed his strategic assignment and had planted the gospel in Africa. But God had fresh fields for His evangelist. No sooner had the Ethiopian been baptized than "the Spirit of the Lord snatched Philip away; and the eunuch saw him no more. . . . But Philip found himself at Azotus; and as he passed through he kept preaching the gospel to all the cities, until he came to Caesarea" (Acts 8:39-40).

Miraculous or Figurative?

There is a divergence of opinion as to whether this passage relates the miraculous intervention of the Spirit or indicates in a graphic way the sudden transferring of Philip to another sphere of service. G. Campbell Morgan wisely said that he was never anxious to read miracles in where they are not, any more than he was anxious to rule miracles out where they were in.[5]

The question at issue is, Does the language used clearly imply miraculous intervention? Greek authority A. T. Robertson says yes. He maintains that Philip was caught away suddenly and miraculously, for the word means "to carry off" (cf. 2 Corinthians 12:2; 1 Thessalonians 4:17).[6]

Evangelist and Host

Under the impulse of the Spirit, the evangelist continued his ministry from Azotus, the ancient Ashdod of the Philistines, to all the cities along the coastal road to Caesarea (Acts 8:40). He thus fulfilled his ministry as a traveling missionary in Samaria, Ethiopia, Azotus, "all the cities," and finally Caesarea.

Throughout the narrative, Philip displays the authentic passion of the evangelist. No ephemeral blaze, the steadily

5. G. Campbell Morgan, *The Acts of the Apostles* (New York: Revell, 1924), p. 218.
6. Archibald Thomas Robertson, *Word Pictures in the New Testament,* 6 vols. (1930-33; reprint ed., Nashville: Broadman, n.d.), vol. 3, *The Acts of the Apostles* (1930), pp. 111-12.

burning flame of his passion was constantly fed by the Holy Spirit. The repeated use of the Greek word *evangelize* reveals the content and subject of his preaching: the Word (Acts 8:4), the Kingdom of God (Acts 8:12), the name of Christ (Acts 8:12), and Jesus (Acts 8:35). Unlike many, Philip did not decline in evangelistic zeal with increasing years, for "he kept preaching the gospel to all the cities" (Acts 8:40).

Our last glimpse of this ardent evangelist is as a generous host, extending hospitality to Paul and Luke, who were doubtless graciously entertained by his four unmarried daughters (Acts 21:8-9).

We are not to understand that these gifted and godly women belonged to a religious order of virgins. They did, however, fulfill a Pentecostal prophecy: "Your daughters shall prophesy" (Acts 2:17). Their ministry did not necessarily involve foretelling the future, although that is not excluded. But from the precedence that Paul accords to the gift, it was obviously something more than ordinary preaching. From Eusebius we learn that at least two of Philip's four daughters lived to a great age,[7] and we may surmise that all four were highly esteemed for the authentic information they could give concerning people and events of the early church. What a blessing a godly family can be to a community!

Variety in Guidance

Philip's varied experiences in the realm of guidance are instructive, for the Holy Spirit is not stereotyped in His methods. The guidance Philip received to leave Jerusalem and go to Samaria was rather unwelcome! "A great persecution arose against the church in Jerusalem. . . . Saul began ravaging the church, entering house after house; and dragging off men and women, he would put them in prison. Therefore, those who had been scattered went about preaching the word. And Philip went down to the city of Samaria" (Acts 8:1, 3-5). His obedience to the voice

7. Eusebius *Ecclesiastical History* 3:31.

of the Spirit in those adverse circumstances opened a door of service.

Next came an unexpected summons through an angelic messenger (Acts 8:26). Prompt obedience opened a continent to the gospel. The inner voice indicated Philip's next sphere of ministry. "The Spirit said to Philip, 'Go up and join this chariot' " (Acts 8:29). The Spirit-filled man recognizes the voice of the Spirit.

Then came the mysterious experience of being snatched away by the Spirit of God (Acts 8:39), and finally we see him exercising his sanctified judgment as he went from city to city en route to Caesarea. With Philip's experiences before us, we should not be surprised if the remarkable experiences in guidance that God occasionally grants are not duplicated. God is amazingly versatile. The spiritually mature are satisfied with quiet guidance.

19

Luke

Doctor Turned Historian

"Luke, the beloved physician" (Colossians 4:14).

"The brother whose fame . . . has spread through all the churches" (2 Corinthians 8:18).

> Luke was never one of the famous figures of the early Church. If he had not written the gospel very certainly no one would have attached it to his name. . . . He was a doctor by profession (Colossians 4:14) and maybe that very fact gave him the wide sympathy that he possessed. It has been said that a minister sees men at their best; a lawyer sees men at their worst; and a doctor sees men as they are. Luke saw men and loved them all.[1]
>
> (William Barclay)

Few unusually gifted authors have been more modest than the one to whom we owe the third gospel. His name appears only three times in the New Testament, and then not from his own pen. In one sense we know less about Luke than any of the other three evangelists. On the other hand, scattered throughout the two books of which he is

1. William Barclay, *The Gospel of Luke,* 2d ed., The Daily Study Bible (Philadelphia: Westminster, 1956), p. xiii.

the author are many self-revealing flashes that tell us a good deal about him.

This is true especially of his gospel. In His inspiration of the Scriptures, the Holy Spirit employed and exploited the unique personalities of the writers in expressing divine truth. In his letters, Paul remains Paul, and his personality is impressed on his writings. Even so with Paul's companion Luke. The personality of the man can, as we shall see, be detected in a score of ways in his skillfully written books.

What we can learn of Luke combines to present a picture of a singularly gifted and lovable character, a man who would at once inspire confidence and win confidences. The overall impression is of a man who is unconsciously great.

Luke's Three Firsts

Luke earned three firsts. He was *the first medical missionary,* the pioneer of that host of dedicated men and women who have devoted their medical knowledge and skill to the alleviation of the physical and spiritual ills of the underprivileged people of the world. His serving as private physician to Paul the missionary in his infirmities made him the first medical missionary to devote himself to the care of the health of his fellow workers.

Then he was *the church's first ecclesiastical historian.* He brought to the task a keen and cultured mind that was married to the meticulous accuracy of the scholar and scientist. The quality of his literary work is very high, according to competent judges. Indeed, his is said to be the best Greek in the New Testament. Ernest Renan, the rationalist, referred to the third gospels as "the most literary of the Gospels" and "the most beautiful book in the world."[2]

As to Luke's qualifications as a historian, Sir William Ramsay, a brilliant authority in that sphere, asserted that Luke had established his right to take his place among the

2. In W. Graham Scroggie, *A Guide to the Gospels* (Westwood, N.J.: Revell, 1948), p. 336.

foremost historians. The value to the church of his contributions cannot be exaggerated, for he preserved for us an authentic history of the young church from its birth until it had spread throughout the Roman Empire.

Luke was *the first Christian hymnologist*. The church is yet further in his debt for his introduction of inspired songs into his history. The first five Christian hymns are found nowhere else: the Ave Maria (Luke 1:42-45), the Magnificat (Luke 1:46-55), the Benedictus (Luke 1:68-79), the Gloria in Excelsis (Luke 2:10-14), and the Nunc Dimittis (Luke 2:29-32).

These lovely songs, composed in heaven, combined to give a worthy symphony of welcome to the Christ Child. Of these hymns, J. M. E. Ross wrote: "There is something in them—how shall we name it? Shall we call it the freshness of the morning or the glow of an unextinguishable fire?—which makes most later hymns seem poor and pale beside them."[3]

At the beginning of Luke's gospel, we read that at the Child's birth a chorus of angelic song swept through the midnight sky (Luke 2:13-14). At the gospel's close, we read of Jesus' disciples returning to Jerusalem with great joy and being continually in the Temple, praising God (Luke 24:52-53). The note of song and praise and joy continually surfaces in Luke's writings.

Versatile in Gift and Achievement

Luke displayed an amazing versatility both in gift and in achievement. There are few in whom a scientific turn of mind goes hand in hand with an artistic temperament, as it does in Luke. Without doubt he was an artist in the use of words, but Nicephorus and others in the tenth century passed on the tradition that he was also no mean artist and had painted portraits of the Lord, Mary, and the chief apostles. How reliable these traditions are is open to ques-

3. J. M. E. Ross, *The Gospel According to St Luke*, 3 vols., Religious Tract Society Devotional Commentary Series (London: Religious Tract Society, n.d.), 1:42-43.

tion, but in the thirteenth century Luke was adopted as the patron saint of painters.

Luke's ability to adapt to the demands of different occasions appears in his literary productions. He readily switched from a scholarly historical style to a more popular, though polished, vernacular. He was equally facile in writing vivid narrative or classical prose. Centuries before psychology was classed among the sciences, and when psychiatry was unknown, Luke displayed an acute insight into the mysteries and idiosyncrasies of the human mind—an insight that betokened careful thought and study.

The Tireless Missionary

Luke's love of song and poetry has been noted, but in addition to those gifts of nature and of grace, he was a tireless missionary. He not only accompanied Paul on many of his journeys, but he also moved among the growing number of churches in which his fame was known and his praises sung (2 Corinthians 8:18). So in this man we see physician, historian, poet, artist, missionary, and loyal friend of the world's greatest missionary.

Both Jerome and Eusebius write of him as hailing from Antioch in Syria, and the weight of evidence is that that was the case. He had the distinction of being the only New Testament writer who was not a Jew. In the fourth century, Eusebius wrote of him: "Luke, who was by race an Antiochian and a physician by profession, was long a companion of Paul, and had careful conversation with the other Apostles, and in two books left us examples of the medicine for souls which he had gained from them."[4]

Three cities were open to Luke for his education and medical training—Alexandria, Athens, and Tarsus. From his association with Paul of Tarsus, the latter is the most probable place of his training. There he could receive an unrivaled classical education, and it may well be that it was there the friends first met. The suggestion has been

4. Eusebius *Ecclesiastical History* 3.4.

made that he may have been a slave of Theophilus, to whom his two books are dedicated.

It was not uncommon in those days for a man of wealth to train a gifted slave in the science of medicine and give him his freedom. That Theophilus was a man of position is clear from the term Luke uses in addressing him: "most excellent Theophilus" (Luke 1:3). A near equivalent in our day would be "your excellency."

As to his conversion to Christianity, there is no authoritative record, but Tertullian ascribes it to the influence of Paul. There is a tradition that before his conversion he had adopted Judaism.

The Beloved Physician

Even if Paul had not written of Luke as "the beloved physician" (Colossians 4:14), his link with medicine could be deduced from the internal evidence of his writings. Dr. Howard A. Kelly, an American professor of medicine who was honored by his fellow Christians with the same title, said in writing of Luke, "His writings carry the hall marks of a medical man in themselves, and his profession is uncontrovertibly embalmed in the very words he uses; we note this especially, as one might readily anticipate, in the technical medical terms he uses as compared with Matthew and with Mark, as well as in his fuller details in describing the miracles of healing; we remark it, too, in describing other events, when in numerous instances he instinctively lays hold of terms for the most part found only in Greek medical authors."[5] He alone preserves for us our Lord's self-appellation, "Physician" (Luke 4:23).

Dr. Kelly points out that in describing the palsied man, Luke used a strictly medical term (Luke 5:18), while Matthew and Mark employed a popular expression for palsy in the same connection. In the account of the woman with the hemorrhage, Luke noted the medical details: it was of twelve years' standing, it had been intractable, and the

5. Howard A. Kelly, "A Doctor's Study of the Doctor's Gospel," *S. S. Times* 73, no. 1 (January 3, 1931):3.

flow of blood was stanched (Luke 8:43-44). The latter phrase is characteristically medical, as shown by the use of the same term by Hippocrates, the father of medicine.

Another intriguing medical touch is seen in the Lord's assertion that "it is easier for a camel to go through the eye of a needle, than for a rich man to enter the kingdom of God" (Luke 18:25). Here Luke used different words from those of the other two synoptists. His word for "needle" means a surgical needle, and his word for "eye" is a medical word for a hole or perforation of any kind in the body. In speaking to the lawyers (Luke 11:46), Jesus said, "You yourselves will not even touch the burdens with one of your fingers." Luke used the word meaning a medical examination of a body by inspection with palpation.

It would appear that Luke used his medical skill on Malta. The father of Publius was cured of recurrent fever and dysentery through Paul's prayers (Acts 28:8). But it is next recorded that "the rest of the people on the island who had diseases were coming to him and getting cured" (Acts 28:9). The statement means that they received medical treatment, presumably from Luke, who was in the party.

It will be seen from these samples of Luke's use of technical medical terms and metaphors that there are unmistakable traces of medical diagnosis and scientific knowledge. Some students have inferred from Luke's interest in seafaring and from his intelligent and accurate reporting of the shipwreck (Acts 27) that he may have served as a ship's doctor.

Distinctive Themes

The themes given prominence in this gospel are characteristic of its author. As *the gospel of the Nativity*, it provides us with the greater part of our knowledge of that sublime event. Some scholars consider that a direct account from the lips of Mary herself may be detected in the Greek form of some sentences recording the birth of Jesus. And who but Mary could have provided the sacred and intimate details Luke recorded with such delicacy?

If Mary were alive at the time of writing, as she may well have been, what is more likely than that this careful historian would go directly to her for the material he desired? In any case, he was associated with members of the apostolic band, and the information could have come through them.

It is also *the gospel of womanhood;* it reflects not only the attitude of our Lord, but also of the author. More than any of the other evangelists, Luke gave prominence to the role and plight of women, and especially widows, in Eastern society. In his writing about womanhood, the innate courtesy and gentleness of the doctor is seen. The respect and attention he paid to women stand out in contrast to the callousness of the men of that day.

When it is remembered that in the Hebrew liturgy the rabbis thanked God that they were not born women, we see that the place Luke accorded to womanhood was distinctly revolutionary. He was at pains to show that Jesus displayed a totally different attitude to the contempt of women manifested by both Jew and pagan.

It is Luke who gave us *the gospel of childhood.* We are indebted to him for the stories of the birth, infancy, and boyhood of both John the Baptist and Jesus. He alone recorded the revealing incident of the boy Jesus' remaining behind in Jerusalem to talk with the rabbis (Luke 2:41-52). What a flood of light those few verses throw upon the nature of our Lord's humanity.

Again, it is *the gospel of the poor* and socially underprivileged. Luke obviously had a strong sense of social responsibility. He seemed almost automatically to champion the cause of the underdog. He delighted to picture Jesus as the Friend of outcasts and sinners—the publican, the prodigal, the penitent thief, the beggar Lazarus. It is Luke who recorded Jesus' appropriation of Isaiah's words for Himself: "He [the Lord] anointed Me to preach the gospel to the poor" (Luke 4:18).

It is *the gospel of prayer.* This is a major theme—especially the prayers that Jesus offered at critical points in His ministry. It is a striking fact that seven of the nine prayers that Luke reproduced were recorded by him alone.

Prayer is the focal point of the vivid parables of the friend at midnight, the unjust judge, and the Pharisee and publican.

Luke evinced a keen interest in *the ministry of angels.* In addition to the twenty-three times angels are mentioned in his gospel, there are nineteen occurrences in the book of Acts. It is therefore to him more than to any other writer that we owe much of our knowledge of angels and the unseen world.

A Choice of Friendship

The association of Luke with Paul was one of the great formative influences of his life. A very deep bond of affection developed between them, and it is not unlikely that it was from Paul that Luke first learned the truths of the gospel. Inevitably this association meant that he was familiar with Paul's views and teaching. Paul was no doubt his hero, and that fact would deeply influence his own views. Irenaeus claimed that Luke "put down in a book the gospel preached by Paul," and that opinion is supported by the similarity of the views and language of both men.

Paul had a great genius for friendship, and his fellowship with Luke was not marred by rupture, as his fellowship with Barnabas had been. Between Luke and Paul there were the warmest mutual appreciation and understanding. It is not difficult to imagine what this comfortable friendship meant to Paul in the midst of his sicknesses and cares.

In this connection, Robert Elliott Speer wrote: "When the care of all the churches and the news of heresy and moral defection lay heavy upon his soul, it must have been a vast relief to Paul to sit down in the genial cheerfulness of Luke's company and be restored by that calm equipose, that patient acceptance of what cannot be helped . . . which fill the atmosphere of every 'beloved physician' with balm and strength."[6]

6. Robert Elliott Speer, *Paul the All-around Man,* 2d ed. (New York: Revell, 1909), p. 186.

The "We" Sections

What are known as the "we" sections of the book of Acts are records of the journeys that Luke took as Paul's companion and personal physician (Acts 16:10-17; 20:4-15; 21:1-18; 27:1—28:16). He first joined Paul at Troas, and he subsequently made several journeys with him. At the close of Paul's detention in Caesarea, Luke accompanied him to Rome and remained with him in his second imprisonment.

The apostle was fortunate in having such a loyal and devoted friend, and he pays tribute to his courageous love and loyalty. Hear the plaintive words of the old warrior: "Demas . . . has deserted me; . . . Crescens has gone to Galatia, Titus to Dalmatia. Only Luke is with me" (2 Timothy 4:10-11).

It is generally agreed that Luke was "the brother whose fame in the things of the gospel has spread through all the churches" (2 Corinthians 8:18). The subscription to the second Corinthian letter sets out that it was "written from Philippi, . . . by Titus and Lucas." The fact of his reputation among "all the churches" being so high gives us a clue to the period during which he was not with Paul—perhaps it was for as long as seven years.

During that period he must have been traveling from place to place among the churches. Knowing what we have learned about him, it is not unrealistic to believe that he had a glorious period of missionary work among the churches he loved.

As to his later years and death, there is little that is undoubtedly authentic. It is not unlikely that he died as a martyr. A passage in Epiphanius states that he preached in Dalmatia, Gallia, Italy, and Macedonia. Gregory Nazianzen first numbered Luke among the martyrs, and Nicephorus records that while ministering in Greece, Luke was hanged on an olive tree, dying unmarried and childless. Whether these traditions are true or not, Luke left behind him a testimony redolent with the fragrance of his Lord.

20

Apollos

The Popular Preacher

"Apollos, . . . an eloquent man, . . . mighty in the Scriptures" (Acts 18:24).

The lack of mighty popular preachers is one of the most alarming signs in the Churches. Where is Apollos? The community recognizes him when he appears, and no amount of booming will permanently persuade the public that one is an Apollos who is not. Eloquence has been God's greatest weapon in days agone, and while humanity is what it is that weapon will retain its supremacy. God perpetuate the influence of heaven-breathed eloquence.[1]

(Dinsdale T. Young)

Apollos was the popular preacher par excellence—eloquent, scholarly, fervent, persuasive. He was a Jew of Alexandria, third city in the Roman Empire. At that time it was the metropolis of Greek culture and learning. It boasted a famous Egyptian library, and being a university city, among its citizens there was a unique blending of Greek, Hebrew, and Oriental culture and philosophy. No city of-

1. Dinsdale T. Young, *Neglected People of the Bible*, 2d ed. (London: Hodder and Stoughton, 1902), p. 248.

fered a more favorable opportunity to acquire a superb education.

Alexandria was also the nerve center of Hellenistic Judaism. The Hellenists were Jews who had been deeply influenced by Greek culture and had adopted Greek as their mother tongue. So Apollos of Alexandria was a man in whom the ideals of both Hebrew and Hellenist were merged.

A Man of Parts

"We meet him [Apollos] first at Ephesus," wrote W. G. Scroggie, "like a blazing comet in the ecclesiastical heavens, striking down opposition and unbelief with the onslaught of his fervid and logical eloquence."[2]

He was a man of parts, and he displayed a rare versatility in his ministry. He was *an eloquent orator*, able to express lofty truth and deep emotions with fluency and persuasiveness. The word "eloquent," as Luke uses it, connotes learning as well as fluency of speech. Apollos's eloquence was not mere verbosity, but the expression of sound scholarship and genuine culture. He could move the crowds with fervid appeals that affected the intellect as well as the emotions. So popular and powerful was his preaching that much to his dismay a personality cult began to develop around him among the fickle, sensation-loving Corinthians.

"Each one of you is saying, 'I am of Paul,' and 'I of Apollos,' and 'I of Cephas'" (1 Corinthians 1:12). Apollos's preaching was probably more colorful than that of Paul the theologian, and one can imagine his admirers urging others: "You must not miss hearing Apollos. I much prefer him to Paul!"

But both Paul and Apollos were distressed that they should be the focus of dissension and division in the church. They strongly disowned this carnal infatuation. When Paul urged Apollos to return to Corinth while he himself remained away (1 Corinthians 16:12), Apollos re-

2. W. Graham Scroggie, *Scripture Union Daily Notes*, June 1929, p. 31.

fused to do so. He did not want to be identified with their factions. His desire was that his God-given eloquence should bring honor to his Master, not that his own popularity should be enhanced.

God is not restricted to eloquence for the proclamation of His evangel; yet it is clear that through the ages He has been pleased to use sanctified rhetoric as one of the most powerful weapons in His armory.

Linked with Apollos's polished rhetorical style, there was *fervency of spirit* (Acts 18:25). "Fervent" means, literally, "boiling in spirit." Coupled with light in his mind was passion in his heart. He was aflame with holy passion. Had he caught some of John the Baptist's fiery zeal? His eloquence and burning logic flowed from the fire in his own heart and imparted a unique quality to his preaching. Scripturally grounded fluency and fervor make an irresistible combination when touched by the Spirit's fire (Acts 6:10).

There is a place for zeal and fervor and enthusiasm in the things of God. Cold preaching may instruct the intellect, but it is unlikely to move the heart and will or stir to holy activity. It is fire we need!

> O Thou who camest from above,
>   The pure celestial fire to impart;
> Kindle a flame of pure desire
>   On the mean altar of my heart.
>   (Charles Wesley)

Mighty in the Scriptures

In addition to his great preaching gift, Apollos was "*mighty in the Scriptures*" (Acts 18:24). As a Hellenist, he would have been especially proficient in the use of the Greek Septuagint version of the Old Testament, which had been translated and published in his own city of Alexandria. His natural gifts enabled him to grasp and understand the letter of the Scriptures, which he had obviously studied deeply. One does not become "mighty" in any realm without diligent application.

The expression "instructed in the way of the Lord" (Acts 18:25) usually signifies oral instruction; it may imply here that he had taken a special oral course of indoctrination. "Instructed" in Greek is the word from which our *catechize* is derived.

It is difficult to discover from the scant Scripture references the extent and nature of his knowledge of gospel truth. As a Jew, he would have been well informed in the Old Testament rituals and Messianic prophecies. Although the phrase "the way of the Lord" may mean "the way of the Lord Jesus," it seems more likely that it refers to Messianic prophecy than to Christianity.

Apollos had already experienced John's baptism of repentance, but apparently he had not learned of Christian baptism or the baptism in the Spirit; he was thus in much the same position as the men of Ephesus (Acts 19:3). We may undoubtedly assume that under the instruction of Aquila and Priscilla and Paul he had accepted Christian baptism and was now filled with the Spirit.

His knowledge of the full content of the gospel message had obviously been deficient, and perhaps defective. He was able to teach "the things concerning Jesus" (Acts 18:25), but this phrase would refer more to the facts of His life and to His moral and ethical teaching than to the deeper truths He shared with His disciples in the upper room. He must have received some authentic teaching about Jesus, however incomplete it was. The important thing to notice is that he shared as much as he knew, and God saw to it that he received more light. Nothing afforded him greater joy than to open and expound the Scriptures.

He was also *a careful expositor* of the Scriptures. Like meticulous Luke, who tells the story, Apollos carefully checked his facts and sources: "He was speaking and teaching accurately the things concerning Jesus" (Acts 18:25). Whether speaking in private or teaching in public, he was equally scrupulous. The Greek verb from which "accurately" comes means "to follow out a subject carefully and thoroughly." He was no slipshod preacher, leaving his sermon preparation until Saturday. Eloquence is good, but it must not be at the expense of accuracy. The truths we present have eternal implications and therefore must not be carelessly presented.

A Popular Apologist

Apollos's preaching was popular and yet courageous, a combination that is not always present. Apollos did not trim his sails to suit his congregation. In full awareness of the opposition his preaching would generate, "he began to speak out *boldly* in the synagogue" (Acts 18:26, italics added). He seemed to thrive on opposition and controversy. There was nothing defensive or apologetic about his presentation; he retained the initiative.

Though not apologetic for his message, he was *an able apologist*, for "he powerfully refuted the Jews in public" (Acts 18:28). He not only presented positive truth, but he also effectively countered the arguments of his opponents. "Refuted" is a very strong word, and the tense gives the meaning "he kept arguing them down," or "he refuted them at every point." The only other occurrence of the word is in Luke 23:10, "The chief priests and the scribes were standing there, accusing Him vehemently." They subjected Jesus to non-Christian vehemence, but Apollos met his opponents with sustained Christian vehemence. He believed his beliefs strongly, and he was prepared to vindicate them to the limit.

His *robust defense of the gospel* was a great strength to the young church at Achaia, which Paul encouraged him to visit. "He helped greatly those who had believed through grace" (Acts 18:27). It meant much to those young Christians to have the assistance of such a doughty champion.

It would appear that he excelled in the art of matching the Messianic prophecies of the Old Testament with their fulfillment in Christ. The Jews had no answer when from their own Scriptures he was able to demonstrate that Jesus was the Messiah for whom they had looked so long. He was able to produce a conclusive counterargument to all their contentions.

The Author of Hebrews?

An interesting sidelight on Apollos's mastery of the Scriptures is thrown by Martin Luther's contention that he was the author of the anonymous letter to the Hebrews. Dean Alford strongly supported this view, which still commands considerable support. But while there are weighty supporting arguments, it has never been finally established.

Luther himself entertained no doubts on the subject. In support of his position, he maintained that whoever the author, like Apollos he was fully familiar with the Alexandrian mode of typical interpretation; he possessed an unusually detailed knowledge of the Old Testament; he was skillful in the use of the Greek language: he thought and argued as would a cultured Alexandrian. Since the letter was written for second-generation Christians, it would be advantageous if the author were one such. It was Luther's contention that Apollos would admirably fill such a specification. From what we can learn of Apollos from available data, he may well have been the author.

There are, however, some adverse factors. None of the church Fathers, who were much closer in time to the events than Luther, has even suggested Apollos's authorship. From earliest times the Christians of Alexandria attributed the letter to another writer—an unlikely procedure had there been any suggestion that one of their honored sons was the author. Then, too, as J. Sidlow Baxter points out, "Apollos was an *Alexandrian* Jew; but does not the Hebrews epistle require a Jew of long and intimate acquaintance with *Jerusalem* and the temple—and with the Jewish Christians there?"[3]

Molding Influences

Without doubt the most formative influence on Apollos's life, not excepting even that of the mighty Paul, was that of

3. J. Sidlow Baxter, *Explore the Book* (Grand Rapids: Zondervan, 1960), vol. 6, *Acts to Revelation*, p. 280.

the two lay workers, Priscilla and Aquila. Because of an oppressive decree of the emperor Claudius, this outstanding Christian couple had been compelled to emigrate from Rome. Coming to Ephesus by way of Corinth, they established a tent-making business, in which Paul joined them and shared their hospitality.

The caliber of these attractive Christians can be gauged by Paul's grateful eulogy: "Greet Prisca and Aquila, my fellow-workers in Christ Jesus, who for my life risked their own necks, to whom not only do I give thanks, but also all the churches of the Gentiles" (Romans 16:3-4). Generous praise this!

Because Priscilla is usually mentioned first in this happy partnership, it has been suggested that she was a woman of high social status; or she may be listed first more often because she was the dominant personality of the team. It is by no means rare that the wife is more able than the husband, and the inspired record draws special attention to the part she played in Apollos's theological education.

When Apollos, also a refugee, came to Ephesus, he gravitated to the synagogue, and before long he was found preaching with uncommon power and fervor. But although he was eloquent and mighty in the Scriptures, the more spiritually mature Priscilla and Aquila detected a missing dimension in his preaching. It was brilliant and moving, but an essential note was lacking. The sensitive way in which they met the situation merits our emulation. Instead of criticizing his lack of enlightenment, they befriended him and took him to their home. What a cheer to a stranger among strangers to be brought into such warm Christian fellowship.

In that congenial atmosphere it was easy and natural for them to supplement his incomplete knowledge of the way of God. He already preached accurately as much as he knew, but they helped him to preach more accurately by remedying the deficiencies in his apprehension of truth.

It says a great deal for *the deep humility* of this brilliant and popular preacher that he did not take umbrage at the two laymen for having the audacity to challenge the adequacy of his message. In the religious climate of those days, it showed no small degree of humility for him to sit at the feet of a woman.

Apollos affords a splendid example of the immense benefit teachable younger Christians may derive from allowing more spiritually mature Christians, even though they may have less academic equipment, to impart their experiential knowledge of the Scriptures and their knowledge of God. What an enduring influence many a godly woman has exerted on a developing Christian worker. Priscilla and Aquila are shining examples of understanding pastoral care for a brilliant protégé. It is much easier to criticize obvious deficiencies than to explain the way of God more perfectly.

There is a tendency today in some circles to downgrade the preaching ministry in favor of dialogue and personal counseling. Necessary and valuable as both dialogue and counseling are in their place in the life of the church, nothing can take the place of authoritative, persuasive, Spirit-anointed preaching. Apollos and his successors still have an honored place in the church. Jesus sent His disciples out to preach. "He ordered us to preach to the people," said Peter (Acts 10:42). The order has not been withdrawn. "I am under compulsion," said Paul; "for woe is me if I do not preach the gospel" (1 Corinthians 9:16).

Apollos was a popular preacher, but it was a popularity that sprang out of a fervent love for Christ and the enduement of the Holy Spirit.

> Then with a rush the intolerable craving
> Shivers throughout me like a trumpet-call,—
> Oh to save these! to perish for their saving,
> Die for their life, be offered for them all![4]
>   (Frederic W. H. Myers)

---

4. Frederic W. H. Myers, *Saint Paul*, 4th ed. (London: Macmillan, 1928), p. 34.